Swami Abhayananda was born Stan Trout in Indianapolis, Indiana on 14 August 1938. In June of 1966 he became acquainted with the philosophy of mysticism and experienced a strong desire to realize God. On 18 November of that same year, by the grace of God, he attained his goal.

He has written a number of books under his own imprint, Atma Books. He founded the Vedanta Temple in Naples, Florida in 1988 and a few years later he reopened the Vedanta Temple in Olympia, Washington, where he now lives and continues to write his works on the knowledge of the Self.

By the same author

History of Mysticism
The Supreme Self: A Modern Upanishad
The Wisdom of Vedanta
*The Origins of Western Mysticism: Selected Writings
of Plotinus*
*Jnaneshvar: The Life and Works of the celebrated
thirteenth-century Indian Mystic-Poet*
Dattatreya's Song of the Avadhut

THOMAS À KEMPIS

ON THE LOVE *of* GOD

A modern rendition of *The Imitation of Christ*

S. ABHAYANANDA

WATKINS PUBLISHING

LONDON

This edition published in the UK in 2004 by
Watkins Publishing, Sixth Floor, Castle House,
75–76 Wells Street, London, W1T 3QH

Designed and typeset by Jerry Goldie
Printed and bound in Great Britain

British Library Cataloguing in Publication data
available

Library of Congress Cataloging in Publication data
available

ISBN 1 84293 063 X

www.watkinspublishing.com

CONTENTS

BOOK TWO:

ADMONITIONS DRAWING TO THE INNER LIFE

BOOK THREE:

THE INWARD SPEAKING OF GOD TO A FAITHFUL SOUL

INTRODUCTION

About Thomas á Kempis

In the late fourteenth century a number of religious communities sprouted up in Europe. Disenchanted with the dry theological hair-splitting of the Scholastics of the preceding century, these communities, made up of the rural populace, wished to return the emphasis of the Christian faith to the holy life of devotion. One such community, called 'The Brethren Of the Common Life', was founded by Gerhard Groot (1340–1384) at Deventer in Holland. This little band of men and women at Deventer was but one of the many that constituted the popular devotional movement known as 'The New Devotion' (*devotio moderne*). There, to Deventer, in 1396, came a young man named Thomas Haemerlein from Kempen on the Rhine, who was to become one of the most beloved and influential saints of all time, known to the world as Thomas á Kempis.

Thomas á Kempis (1380–1471) entered The Brethren Of The Common Life at the age of sixteen, was educated in that community, and at the age of twenty-two became a monk of the

Augustine Canons at the monastery of Mount Saint Agnes in Zwolle, near Utrecht. There he lived, totally obscured to the world, for seventy years, until his death on July 26, 1471. His daily work for many years was the artful copying of manuscripts, and his daily intent was to God, so that he might be continually in awareness of His presence. In the days he worked, and in the nights he prayed and wrote. He was eventually made Director of Novitiates, and in this capacity guided the novices in spiritual life through the snares and pitfalls on the path to blessedness in God.

In his solitary nights, Thomas wrote down his interior meditations and prayers, and these pure outflowings of God's activity in him were eventually collected in the form of a small book to be shared with his novices in the interest of their spiritual welfare. In a very short time after his death, however, his little book was frequently copied and widely circulated, not only among his fellow ecclesiastics, but among the lay populace as well; and it was immediately received as a supremely holy book of spiritual guidance. As the earliest Latin manuscripts of this book were untitled as well as unsigned, for purposes of identification it was circulated under the title, *Musica Ecclesiastica*, or 'Music Of The Church'; but later copiers, forming a title for it from the first few words of the opening chapter, called it, *De Imitatio Christi*, or 'Of The Imitation Of Christ'. It is by that name that it is known to us today.

Because the book was unsigned, and its author indifferent to fame, there is no way to be absolutely certain that *The Imitation Of Christ* was the work of Thomas á Kempis; but until it is proven otherwise, he is considered to be its author. Thomas wrote a few other works, including a biography of Gerhard Groot, the founder of The Brethren Of The Common Life, but this one little book of spiritual counsels, known as *The Imitation Of Christ,* remains the primary work for which he is justly remembered and revered. It is one of a very few universally beloved classics, as much honored and loved by non-Christians as by Christians, and held by many to be the most holy and perfect guide to the devotional life ever created.

About His Book

In one form or another, Thomas' little book has been published throughout the world more often than any other book except the Holy Bible. And, while it is a Christian book written by a Christian author, its appeal goes far beyond the narrow confines of sectarian religion. To Christians, it is a testimony of the Christian faith, but to contemplatives of every land and every religious affiliation, it is a universally beloved classic of devotion to God. It is in recognition of its universal significance and appeal that it is now being presented in this revised and non-sectarian edition. It is intended for men and women of all religious persuasions who treasure and savor the sweet words of all true enlightened saints and lovers of God.

Originally written in Latin, *De Imitatio Christi* was translated into English circa 1530 by Richard Whitford (1476–1542). The present edition, retitled *On The Love Of God*, is a revised and edited rendition of that magnificent English translation. It has been altered only insofar as it was necessary to modernize certain archaic idioms, and to delete certain passages or chapters comprised of exclusively sectarian doctrines. The result is a book of truly universal application, a non-sectarian handbook of spiritual contemplation, relevant to all true seekers of God.

On The Love Of God is fashioned in three 'Books', each leading to a progressively more interior state than the one before: in the First, the stage is set in preparing the aspirant for contemplation by freeing his mind from all exterior concerns; in the Second, the aspirant is turned to the interior examination of his own soul; and the Third leads the purified aspirant on his upward journey, by the way of loving surrender at the feet of God. The author's timeless counsels on the path to God are as meaningful today as ever. His voice is the archetypical voice of the soul yearning for the pure Being of its own depths, the

Godhood which is always its true and eternal Self. Such prayerful longing is God's own voice of longing for His eternal state; and this longing resides in the human breast as the eternal legacy of all peoples of every time and persuasion.

The author of this book had experienced that 'Unity' of which he spoke; he had been graced with 'the vision of God', and continued to seek the recurrence of this vision throughout his life. Evidence of this may clearly be seen by those who, themselves have known this 'vision', and are therefore able to recognize it in the author's writings, though his modesty and the constraints demanded by the times prevented him from speaking explicitly of it.

Throughout his book, Thomas carries on a prayerful dialogue with God, leading some to think that he maintained a separation between his own soul and God; but he was intimately familiar with the fact of his existence in God. He was also aware that the dialogue between the individualized soul and God must exist only so long as the soul exists. But when the soul is lifted up in consciousness, by God's grace, it becomes merged and dissolved in the Oneness of God. When this occurs, there is no more dialogue; there is only the one infinite Self. From that singular perspective, all devotional dialogue appears foolish and irrelevant, even ludicrous, for the duality of soul and God is no more, and from that eternal perspective, the one 'I' is all that truly is, or was, or ever will be.

And yet the pure transparence of the soul by which it becomes likened to God, and fit for that incomparable grace, is accomplished only by the selfless love of God. That selfless love expressed by Thomas á Kempis is the *ladder* by which the soul reaches that rare ascension. And so, in the world of men, in the realm of duality in which most of us live, where souls yet stand apart from their Source, this humble and prayerful dialogue between the soul and its God is the highest and most worthy of practices, for it represents the highest possible state of the soul prior to its dissolution in the heart of God. And this rare and divine book is its most eloquent and exquisite expression, capable of leading those who identify with its voice to that same experience of unity.

This amazing and wonderful book has often been criticized by the worldly for its apparent negation of the world; for it repeatedly refers to the 'despising of the world', the need for solitary prayer and meditation, and the restraint of the senses. And it is quite true that this book is of no value whatever to those whose aims are centered solely in worldly satisfactions; it is addressed to those whose aim is the experiential knowledge of oneness with that eternal Source who transcends the world.

Therefore, Thomas' book may not truly be judged according to the purposes of ordinary men, but only according to whether or not it is appropriate to its own avowed purpose: the preparation of the soul for the fulfillment of its desire for union with God. Judged on this basis, this book has been proven time and time again by countless practicing contemplatives to be a most perfectly appropriate and trustworthy guide. It has been the special solace of renunciants and scholars, popes and laymen, statesmen and kings, for over five centuries. And to me, also, it has proven itself to be an inestimable treasure, a marvellous and magical source of inspiration and joy.

It is this very book which has served, since the beginning of my spiritual life, as my most trusted guide and incessant nightly companion. I cannot express the value that it has had to me and continues to have in my life. After a long and thorough search of the world's greatest devotional literature, this book continues to be, for me, the most perfect, most sublime, most divine book in existence. I recommend and urge its *repeated* study to anyone who wishes to prepare himself for the meeting with God.

S. Abhayananda

BOOK ONE:

ADMONITIONS
USEFUL FOR A
SPIRITUAL LIFE

CHAPTER I

Of The Despising Of All The Vanities Of The World

All that is in this world is vanity, but to love God and to serve only Him. This is the most noble and most excellent wisdom that may be in any creature, by despising of this world to draw daily nearer and nearer to the kingdom of God.

It is therefore a great vanity to labor inordinately for worldly riches that shortly shall perish, and to covet honor or any other inordinate pleasures or fleshly delights in this world, whereby a man after this life shall be sorely and grievously punished. How great a vanity is it also to desire a long life, and little to care for a good life; to heed things present, and not to provide for things that are to come; to love things that shortly shall pass away, and not to hasten thither where is joy everlasting.

Have this common proverb often in your mind: 'The eye is not satisfied nor fully pleased with the sight of any bodily thing, nor the ear with hearing'. Therefore study to withdraw the love of your soul from all things that are visible and turn it to things that are invisible; for they who follow their sensuality hurt their own conscience and lose the grace of God.

CHAPTER II

Against Vain Learning And Of A Meek Knowing Of Ourselves

Every man naturally desires to know, but what avails knowledge without the fear of God? A humble farmer who serves God is more acceptable to Him than is a curious philosopher who, considering the course of the heavens, wilfully forgets himself. He who well knows himself is vile and abject in his own sight and has no delight in the vain praisings of man. If I knew all things in this world, without love, what should it avail me before God who judges every man according to his deeds? Let us therefore cease from the desire of such vain knowledge, for oftentimes is found therein great distraction and deceit, whereby the soul is much hindered and withheld from the perfect and true love of God.

They who have great learning desire commonly to be seen and to be held wise in the world. There are many things the knowledge of which brings but little profit and little fruit to the soul, and he is very unwise who takes heed to any other thing than to that which shall profit him to the health of his soul. Words feed not the soul, but a good life refreshes the mind and a clean conscience brings a man to a firm and stable trust in God. The more knowledge you have, if you live not thereafter, the more grievously shall you be judged for the misusing thereof. Therefore raise not yourself unto pride for any craft or knowledge that is given to you, but have the more fear and dread in your heart, for certain it is that you must hereafter yield therefor the stricter account.

If you think that you know many things and have great learning, then know for certain that there are many more things that you do not know. And so you may not rightly think yourself learned but ought rather to confess your ignorance and folly. Why will you prefer yourself in knowledge before another, since there are many others more excellent and more wise than you, and better learned in the law? If you would learn and know anything profitable to the health of your soul, learn to be unknown and be glad to be held vile and unwise as you are.

The most high and the most profitable learning is this, that a man have a true knowledge and a full despising of himself. Also not to presume of himself, and always to judge and to think well and blessedly of others, is a sign and a token of great wisdom, and of great perfection and singular grace. If you see any person sin or commit any great crime openly before you, yet judge not yourself to be better than he, for you know not how long you shall persevere in goodness. We are all frail, but you should judge no man more frail than yourself.

CHAPTER III

Of The Teaching Of Truth

Happy and blessed is that person whom Truth teaches and informs, not by images or by deceitful voices, but as the Truth is. Our opinion and our wit many times deceive us, for we see not the truth. What avails us the knowledge of such things as shall neither help us to the attainment of God if we know them, nor hinder us if we know them not?

It is therefore great folly to be negligent in such things as are profitable and necessary to us, and to labor for such things as are but curious and damnable. Truly, if we do so, we have eyes but we see not. And what avails us the knowledge of the kind and working of creatures? Truly nothing. He to whom the everlasting Truth speaks is discharged of many vain opinions. Of Him all things proceed and all things openly show and cry that He is God. No man without Him understands the truth nor rightfully judges. But he to whom all things are One, and who draws all things into One, and sets all things in One, and desires but One, may soon be stable in heart and be fully pacified in God.

O Truth that God art, make me one with Thee in perfect love, for all that I read, hear, or see, without Thee is grievous to me; for in Thee is all that I will or may desire. Let all the learned be still in Thy presence, and let all creatures keep themselves in silence, and Thou only, Lord, speak to my soul. The more that a man is made one with Thee and the more that he is gathered together in Thee, the more he understands without labor high secret mystreries, for he has received from above the light of understanding.

A clean, pure, and stable heart is not broken nor easily overcome with spiritual labors, for he does all things to the honor of God; and because he is clearly mortified to himself, therefore he covets to be free from following his own will. What hinders you more than your own affections not fully mortified to the will of the Spirit? Truly, nothing more. A good devout man so orders his outward business that it draw him not to the love of it, but that he compel it to be obedient to the will of the Spirit and to the right judgement of reason. Who has a stronger battle than he who labors to overcome himself? And it should be our daily labor and our daily desire to overcome ourselves, that we may be made stronger in Spirit and increase daily from better to better.

Every perfection in this life has some imperfection attached to it, and there is no knowledge in this world that is not mixed with some blindness of ignorance. And therefore a meek knowing of ourselves is a more certain way to God than is the searching for highness of learning.

Learning well-ordered is not to be blamed, for it is good and comes from God; but a clean conscience and a virtuous life is much better and more to be desired. Because some men study to have learning rather than to live well, they err many times and bring forth little good fruit, or none. O if they would be as busy to avoid sin and to plant virtues in their souls as they are to dispute questions, there would not be so many evil things seen in the world, nor so much evil example given to the people, nor yet so much dissolute living in religion. Our Lord shall not ask of us what we have read, but what we have done; not how well we have said, but how religiously we have lived.

Tell me, where now are all the great writers and famous doctors whom you have well known? When they lived they flourished greatly in their learning, and now other men occupy their positions and offices and I cannot tell whether they think anything on them. In their lifetimes they were held great in the world and now there is little spoken of them. O how shortly passes away the glory of this world with all the false deceitful pleasures of it. Would to God their lives had accorded well with their learning, for then had they well studied and read! How many perish daily in this world by vain learning who care little for a good life and for the service of God; and because they desired rather to be great in the world than to be meek, they vanish away in their learning as smoke in the air.

Truly he is great who has great love, and he is great who is little in his own sight and who regards as nothing all worldly honor. And he is very wise who accounts all worldly pleasures as vile dung, so that he may win God, and he is very well taught who forsakes his own will and follows the will of God.

CHAPTER IV

That Credence Is Not To Be Readily Given To Words

It is not good readily to believe every word or instinct that comes, but the thing is advisedly and leisurely to be considered and pondered, so that almighty God may not be offended through our instability. But alas for sorrow, we are so frail that we believe of others evil sooner than good. Nevertheless, perfect men are not so credulous for they know well that the frailty of man is more prone to evil than to good, and that he is in words very unstable. It is therefore great wisdom not to be hasty in our deeds, not to trust much in our own wits, not readily to believe every tale nor forthwith to show to others all that we hear or believe.

Take always counsel of a wise man and covet rather to be instructed and to be ordered by others than to follow your own invention. A good life makes a man wise towards God, and instructs him in many things that a sinful man shall never feel nor know. The more meek that a man is in himself and the more obedient that he is to God, the more wise and the more peaceful shall he be in eveything that he shall have to do.

CHAPTER V

Of Inordinate Affections

When a man desires anything inordinately, forthwith he is inquiet in himself. The proud man and the covetous man never have rest, but the meek man and the poor in spirit live in great abundance of rest and peace.

A man who is not yet mortified to himself is easily tempted and overcome in little and small temptations. And he who is weak in spirit and is yet somewhat carnal and inclined to outward things may hardly withdraw himself from worldly desires; and when he does withdraw himself from them he has often great grief and heaviness in heart therefor, and he is quickly disdainful if any man resist him. And if he obtains that which he desires, still he is inquieted with grudge of conscience for he has followed his passion which in no way helps to getting of the peace that he desired.

Then, by resisting of passions is gotten the very true peace of heart and not by following of them. There is therefore no peace in the heart of a carnal man, nor in the heart of a man who gives himself entirely to outward things. But in the hearts of spiritual men and women, who have their delight in God, is found great peace and inward quietness.

CHAPTER VI

That Vain Hope And Elation Of Mind Are To Be Fled And Avoided

He is vain who puts his trust in man or in any created thing. Be not ashamed to serve others for the love of God, and to be poor in this world for His sake. Trust not in yourself, but all your trust set in God. So long as in you is the desire to please Him, He shall well help forth your good will. Trust not in your own wisdom nor yet in the wisdom or policy of any creature living, but rather in the grace of God, who helps meek persons, and allows those who presume of themselves to fall till they become meek. Glorify not yourself in your riches nor in your worldly friends because they are powerful; but let all your glory be in God alone who gives all things and who desires to give Himself above all things.

Exalt not yourself for your largeness or fairness of body, for with a little sickness it may be soon defouled. Joy not in yourself for your ability or readiness of wit lest you displease God, of whose gift is all that you have. Hold not yourself better than others, lest perhaps you be thereby impaired in the sight of God, who knows all that is in man. Be not proud of your good deeds; for the judgements of God are other than the judgements of man, and that which pleases man oftentimes displeases God. If you have any goodness or virtue in you, believe yet that there is much more goodness and virtue in others; so that you may always keep yourself in meekness. It hurts not if you hold yourself worse than any other, though it may not be so indeed; but it hurts much if you prefer yourself above any other, though he be the greatest of sinners. Great peace is with the meek man, but in the heart of a proud man is always envy and indignation.

CHAPTER VII

That Much Familiarity Is To Be Fled

Open not your heart to every person, but only to him who is wise, discreet, and dreading God. Be seldom with strangers, flatter not rich men, and before great men do not readily appear. Accompany yourself with meek persons who are simple in heart, devout and of good governance, and treat with them of things that may edify and strengthen your soul. Be not familiar to any woman, but all good women commend to God. Covet to be familiar only with God and with His angels; but the familiarity of man, as much as you may, see that you avoid. Charity is to be had to all, but familiarity is not expedient.

Sometimes it happens that a person unknown, through his good fame, is much commended, whose presence afterwards we like not so much. And we think sometimes with our presence to please others, when we rather displease them through the evil manners and evil conditions that they see and consider to be in us.

CHAPTER VIII

That We Should Avoid Superfluity Of Words And The Company Of Worldly Living People

Flee the company of worldly-living people as much as you may, for the treating of worldly matters hinders greatly the fervor of spirit though it may be done with a good intent. We are quickly deceived with vanity of the world and enslaved to it unless we take good heed.

I wish I had held my peace many times when I have spoken, and that I had not been so much among worldly company as I have been. But why are we so glad to speak and commune together, since we so seldom depart without some hurt of conscience? This is the cause: by our communing together we think to comfort each other and to refresh our hearts when we are troubled with vain imaginations; and we speak most gladly of those things we most love, or else of those things that are most contrarious to us. But alas for sorrow, all is vain that we do, for this outward comfort is no little hindrance to the true inward comfort that comes of God.

Therefore, it is necessary that we watch and pray that the time pass not away from us in idleness. If it is lawful and expedient to speak, speak then of God and of such things as are to the edifying of your soul or of your neighbor's. An evil use and a negligence of spiritual profit makes us oftentimes to take little heed how we should speak. Nevertheless a devout communing of spiritual things sometimes helps very much to the health of the soul, especially when men of one mind and of one spirit in God do meet, and speak, and commune together.

Chapter IX

Of The Means To Get Peace, And Of The Desire To Profit In Virtues

We might have much peace if we would not meddle with other men's sayings and doings that do not belong to us. How may he long live in peace who wilfully meddles with other men's business, and who seeks occasions outwardly in the world and seldom or never gathers himself together in God? Blessed are the true, simple, and meek persons, for they shall have great plenty of peace.

Why have many saints been so perfectly contemplative? Because they always studied to mortify themselves from worldly desires, that they might freely, with all the power of their heart, tend to our

Lord. But we are occupied with our passions and are much busied with transitory things, and it is very seldom that we may fully overcome any one vice. And we are not at all quick to our daily duties, wherefore we remain cold and slow to devotion. If we were perfectly mortified to the world and to the flesh, and were inwardly purified in soul, we should more often savor heavenly things and somewhat should we have experience of heavenly contemplation.

The greatest hindrance of heavenly contemplation is that we are not yet clearly delivered from our passions and lusts. We enforce not ourselves to follow the way that holy saints have gone before us, but when any little adversity comes to us we are quickly cast down therein and turn ourselves too readily to the seeking of man's comfort. But if we would, as strong men and as mighty champions, fight strongly in this spiritual battle, we should undoubtedly see the help of God come in our need, for He is always ready to help all those who trust in Him. And He procures occasions of such battle so that we may overcome and get the victory, and in the end have the greater reward therefor.

If we place the end and perfection of our religion in outward observances, our devotion shall soon be ended; wherefore we must set our axe deep to the root of the tree, that, purged from all passions, we may have a quiet mind. If we would every year overcome one vice, we should quickly come to perfection; but I fear rather that, contrariwise, we were better and purer in the beginning of our conversion than we are many years after we were converted. Our fervor and desire to virtue should daily increase in us as we increase in age, but it is now thought a great thing if we may hold a little spark of the fervor that we had first. If we would at the beginning break the evil inclination that we have to ourselves and to our own will, we should afterwards do virtuous works easily and with great gladness of heart.

If you do not overcome small and light things, how shall you then overcome the greater? Therefore, quickly resist your evil inclinations in the beginning, and leave off wholly all your evil customs lest perhaps, by little and little, they bring you afterwards to greater difficulty. O if you would consider how great inward peace you should have yourself, and how great gladness you should cause in others, in behaving of yourself well, I suppose, truly, you would be much more diligent to profit in virtue than you have been before this time.

CHAPTER X

Of The Profit Of Adversity

It is good that we sometimes have griefs and adversities; for they drive a man to behold himself and to see that he is here as but an exile, and to learn thereby that he ought not to put his trust in any worldly thing. It is good also that we sometimes suffer contradiction, and that we are held by others as evil and wretched and sinful, though we do well and intend well, for such things help us to meekness, and mightily defend us from vainglory and pride. We take God the better to be our judge and witness when we are outwardly despised in the world and when the world judges not well of us. Therefore a man ought to establish himself so fully in God that whatsoever adversity befalls unto him he shall not need to seek any outward comfort.

When a good man is troubled or tempted, or is inquieted with evil thoughts, then he understands and knows that God is most necessary to him and that he may do nothing that is good without Him. Then he sorrows, wails, and prays because of the miseries that he rightfully suffers. Then irks him, also, the wretchedness of this life, and he covets to be dissolved from this body of death and to be with God; for he sees that there may be no full peace nor perfect security here in this world.

Chapter XI

Of Temptations To Be Resisted

There is no man so perfect nor so holy in this world that he has not at some time temptations, and we may not fully be without them; for though they are for the time very grievous and painful, yet if they are resisted they are very profitable. For by them a man is made more meek, and is purged and informed in diverse manners which he should never have known but by experience of such temptations.

There is no Order so holy nor any place so secret that it is fully without temptation, and there is no man who is fully safe from it here in this life; for in our corrupt body we bear that whereby we are tempted, that is, the inordinate lusts with which we were born. As one temptation goes another comes, and so we shall always have somewhat to suffer; and the cause is that we are yet susceptible to the desires of the flesh.

Many persons seek to flee temptation and they fall the more grievously into it. For we may not have victory merely by fleeing, but by meekness and patience we are made stronger than all our enemies. He who only flees the outward occasions and does not cut away the inordinate desires hid inwardly in the heart, shall little profit; and temptations shall readily come to him again and grieve him more than they did first. By little and little, with patience and with sufference, and with help of God, you shall sooner overcome temptations than with your own strength and importunity. In your temptation it is good that you often ask counsel and that you be not rigorous to any person who is tempted, but be glad to comfort him as you would be comforted.

The beginning of all evil temptations is inconstance of mind and too little a trust in God. For as a ship without a rudder is driven hither and thither with every storm, so an unstable man who readily leaves his good purpose in God is diversely tempted. As fire proves gold, temptation proves the righteous man.

We know not, many times, what we can suffer, but temptation shows plainly what we are and what virtue is in us. It is necessary in the beginning of every temptation to be well wary, for the evil propensity is readily overcome if it is not allowed to enter into the heart, but is resisted and shut out as soon as it proffers to enter. For as a bodily medicine is very late administered when the sickness has been allowed to increase by long continuance, so it is of temptation: first comes to the mind an unclean thought and after follows a strong imagination, then delectation and diverse evil motions, and in the end follows a full assent. And so little by little, the evil inclination has full entrance, for it was not wisely resisted in the beginning. The more slow that a man is in resisting, the weaker he is to resist, and the evil propensity is daily the stronger against him.

Some persons have their greatest temptations in the beginning of their conversion, some in the end; some are troubled therewith all their lifetime, and there are many who are easily tempted. All this comes of the great wisdom of God, who knows the state and merit of every person, and ordains all things for the best and for the everlasting health and salvation of His elect and chosen people. Therefore, we shall not despair when we are tempted, but shall the more fervently pray unto God, that of His infinite goodness and fatherly pity He consent to help us in every need; and that He so prevent us with His grace in every temptation, that we shall be able to endure. Let us then humble our souls under the strong hand of almighty God, for He will save and exalt all those here who are meek and low in spirit.

In temptations and tribulations a man is proved how much he has profited, and his merit is thereby the greater in the sight of God, and his virtues the more openly shown. It is no great marvel if a man is fervent and devout when he feels no grief, but if he can suffer patiently in the time of temptation or other adversity, and therewithal can stir himself also to fervor of spirit, it is a token that he shall greatly profit hereafter in virtue and grace. Some persons are kept from any great temptations and yet daily they are overcome through little and small occasions, so that they shall not trust nor presume of themselves who see themselves so easily and in so little things daily overcome.

CHAPTER XII

That We Shall Not Hastily Judge Other Men's Deeds Nor Cleave Much To Our Own Will

Have always a good eye to yourself and be wary that you do not hastily judge other men. In judging others a man often labors in vain, often errs, and easily offends God; but in judging himself and his own deeds he always labors fruitfully and to his spiritual profit.

We judge oftentimes according to our own heart and our own affections and not according to the truth, for we lose the true judgement through our private love. If God were always the whole intent of our desire we should not so hastily err in our judgements nor be so readily troubled because we are resisted of our will; but commonly there is in us some inward inclination or some outward affection that draws our heart with them from the true judgement.

Many persons, through a secret love that they have for themselves, work indiscreetly according to their own will and not according to the will of God, and yet they know it not. They seem to stand in great inward peace when things follow according to their own mind, but if it follow otherwise than they would, quickly they are moved with impatience and are very heavy and pensive.

By diversity of opinions are sprung many times dissension between friends and neighbors, and also between religious and devout persons. An old custom is not easily broken, and no man will readily be moved from his own will; but if you cleave more to your own will or to your own reason than to the meek obedience of truth, it will be long before you are a man illumined with grace. For almighty God wills that we be perfectly subject and obedient to Him and that we rise high above our own will and above our own reason by a great burning love and a whole desire to Him.

CHAPTER XIII

Of Works Done Out Of Love

For nothing in the world, nor for the love of any created thing, is evil to be done. But sometimes for the need and comfort of our neighbor a good deed may be deferred, or be turned into another good deed; for thereby the good deed is not destroyed but is changed into better.

Without love, the outward deed is little to be praised; but whatsoever is done of love, be it never so little or never so despisable in the eyes of the world, it is very profitable before God, who judges all things according to the intent of the doer and not according to the greatness or worthiness of the deed. He does much who much loves God; and he does much who does his deed well; and he does his deed well who does it rather for the community than for his own will. A deed sometimes seems to be done out of love of God when it is rather done of a carnality, and of a fleshly love, than of a charitable love. For commonly some carnal inclination to our friends, some inordinate love to ourselves, some hope of a temporal reward or desire of some other profit, moves us to do the deed, and not the pure love of God.

Love seeks not himself in what he does, but he desires to do only that which shall be honor and praising to God. He envies no man, for he loves no private love. He will not joy in himself but he covets above all things to be blessed in God. He knows well that no goodness begins originally of man, and therefore he refers all goodness to God, of whom all things proceed and in whom all blessed saints rest in everlasting fruition. O he who had a little spark of this perfect love should feel of a certainty in his soul that all earthly things are full of vanity!

Chapter XIV

Of The Suffering Of Other Men's Faults

Such faults as we cannot amend in ourselves or in others we must patiently suffer till our Lord of His goodness will otherwise dispose. And we shall think that perhaps it is best so to be, for the proving of our patience, without which our merits are but little to be pondered. Nevertheless you should pray heartily that our Lord of His great mercy and goodness consent to help us that we may patiently bear such impediments.

If you admonish any person once or twice and he will not take it, strive not overmuch with him but commit all to God, that His will be done and His honor acknowledged in all His servants; for

He can well by His goodness turn evil into good. Study always that you be patient in suffering of other men's faults, for you have many things in yourself that others do suffer of you, and if you cannot make yourself to be as you would, how may you then look to have another to be ordered in all things according to your will?

We would gladly have others perfect, but we will not amend our own faults. We would that others should be strictly corrected for their offences, but we will not be corrected. We dislike it that others have liberty, but we will not be denied of that which we ask. We would that others should be restrained according to the laws, but we will in no way be restrained. Thus it appears evident that we seldom ponder our neighbor as we do ourselves.

If all men were perfect, what had we then to suffer from our neighbors for God? Therefore God has so ordained that each one of us shall learn to bear another's burden; for in this world no man is without fault, no man without burden, no man sufficient to himself, and no man wise enough of himself. Wherefore it behoves each one of us to bear the burden of others, to comfort others, to help others, to counsel others, and to instruct and admonish others in the spirit of love. Who is of most virtue appears best in time of adversity. Occasions make not a man frail, but they show openly what he is.

CHAPTER XV

What Should Be The Life Of A True Religious Person

It behoves you to break your own will in many things if you will have peace and concord with others. It is no little thing to be in monasteries or in congregations, to continue there without complaining or gainsaying, and faithfully to persevere there unto the end. Blessed are they who live there well and make a good end. If you will stand surely in grace and much profit in virtue, hold yourself as an exile and as a pilgrim here in this life, and be glad, for the love of God, to be held in the world as a fool and a vile person, as you are.

The donning of religious clothing helps little, but the changing of life and the mortifying of passions makes a person perfectly and truly religious. He who seeks any other thing in religion than God and the health of his soul, shall find nothing there but trouble and sorrow; and he may not stand long there in peace and quietness who does not labor to be least and subject to all.

It is good, therefore, that you remember often that you came to religion to serve, and not to be served. and that you are called thither to suffer and to labor, and not to be idle nor to tell vain tales. In religion a man shall be proved as gold in a furnace, and no man may stand long there in grace and virtue unless he will, with all his heart, humble himself for the love of God.

CHAPTER XVI

Of The Examples Of Holy Fathers

Behold the lively examples of holy fathers and blessed saints in whom flourished and shone all true perfection of life and all perfect religion, and you shall see how little it is, and next to nothing, that we do now in these days in comparison with them.

O what is our life if it is compared to theirs! They served our Lord in hunger and in thirst, in heat, in cold, in nakedness, in labor and in weariness, in vigils and fastings, in prayers and in holy meditations, in persecutions, and in many reproofs.

O how many and how grievous were the tribulations suffered by all the holy saints! They refused honors and all bodily pleasures here in this life that they might always have the everlasting life. O how strict and abject a life led the holy fathers in the wilderness! What grievous temptations they suffered, how fiercely they were assailed by the clamorings of the flesh! How fervent the prayer they daily offered to God, what rigorous abstinence they used, how great zeal and fervor they had to spiritual profit, how strong a battle they waged against all sin, and how pure and whole an intent they had to God in all their deeds.

In the day they labored and in the night they prayed. And though they labored in the day bodily yet they prayed in mind; and so they spent their time always fruitfully. They thought every hour short for the service of God; and for the great sweetness that they had in heavenly contemplation they forgot oftentimes their bodily refection. All riches, honor, dignities, kinsmen and friends, they renounced for the love of God. They coveted to have nothing of the world, and scarcely would they take that which was necessary for their fleshly nourishment.

They were poor in worldly goods but they were rich in grace and virtue; they were needy outwardly, but inwardly in their souls they were replenished with grace and spiritual comforts. To the world they were aliens and strangers, but to God they were very dear and familiar friends. In the sight of the world and in their own sight they were vile and abject, but in the sight of God and of His saints they were precious and singularly elect. In them shone all perfection of virtue, true meekness, simple obedience, charity, and patience, with other similar virtues and gracious gifts of God; wherefore they profited daily in spirit and obtained great grace of God. They remain as an example to all religious persons, and more ought their lives to stir us to devotion, and to profit us more and more in virtue and grace, than the example of dissolute and idle persons should in any way draw us backward.

O what fervor we have seen in the lives of religious persons; what devotion in prayers, what zeal to virtue, what love for spiritual discipline; and what reverence and meek obedience flourished in them under the rule of their superior. Truly, their deeds yet bear witness that they were holy and perfect who so mightily subdued the world and thrust it under foot.

Nowadays, he is accounted virtuous who is not an offender, and who may with patience keep some little spark of that virtue and of that fervor that he had at first. But alas for sorrow, it is through our own sloth and negligence, and through the losing of time, that we are so soon fallen from our first fervor into such a spiritual weakness and dullness of spirit that it is almost too tedious to us to live. Would to God that the desire to profit in virtue slept not so utterly in us, who so often have seen the holy example of blessed saints.

Chapter XVII

Of The Exercises Of A Good Religious Person

The life of a good religious man should shine in all virtue and be inwardly as it appears outwardly. And the much more inwardly, for almighty God beholds the heart, and we should always honor and reverence Him, and appear before Him as angels, clean and pure, shining in all virtue.

We ought every day to renew our purpose in God and to stir our hearts to fervor and devotion, as though it were the first day of our conversion, and daily to pray and say thus: 'Help me, Lord, that I may persevere in good purpose and in Thy holy service unto my death; and that I may now, this present day, perfectly begin, for it is nothing that I have done in time past.'

According to our purpose and according to our intent shall be our reward. And though our intent be never so good, yet it is necessary that we put thereto a good will and a great diligence; for if he who oftentimes intends to do well and to profit in virtue yet fails in his doing, what then shall another do who seldom or never takes such purpose? Though we may intend to do the best we can, yet our good purpose may happen to be hindered in diverse manners. And our special hindrance is that we so readily leave off our good exercises that we used to do before; for it is seldom seen that a good custom wilfully broken may be recovered again without great spiritual hindrance. The purpose of righteous men depends on the grace of God more than in themselves or in their own wisdom; for man purposes but God disposes, and the way that man shall walk in this world is not in himself but in the grace of God.

If a good custom is sometimes left off in order to help our neighbor it may soon be recovered, but if it is left off through sloth or through negligence of ourselves it will hinder us greatly, and hardly will it be recovered again. Thus it appears that though we encourage ourselves all that we can to do well, yet we shall often fail in many things. And nevertheless though we may not always fulfill it, yet it is good that we always take such good purpose, especially against such things as hinder us most.

We must also make diligent search, both within and without, that we leave nothing inordinate unreformed in us, as much as our frailty may allow; and if you cannot, for frailty of yourself, do thus continually, yet at the least see that you do it once in the day, evening or morning. In the morning you should take a good purpose for that day following, and at night you should examine diligently how you have behaved yourself in word, in deed, and in thought; for in them we do often offend God and our neighbor.

Arm yourself as a true knight with meekness and charity against all the malice of your own evil inclinations. Refrain gluttony, and you shall the more easily refrain all carnal desires. Do not be found entirely idle, but take heed that you are always reading, writing, praying devoutly, thinking, or doing some other good labor for the community.

Bodily exercises are to be done discreetly, for that which is profitable to one is sometimes hurtful to another. And also spiritual labors done of devotion are more surely done in private than in a public place. All may not use one manner of exercise, but one in one manner, another in another manner, as they shall feel to be most profitable to them. Also as the time requires, so diverse exercises are to be used; for one manner of exercise is necessary on one occasion, another at a different time; one in time of temptation, another in time of peace and consolation; one when we have sweetness in devotion, another when devotion withdraws.

Also there are times when we need to be more diligent in good works than at other times; to call devoutly for help to the blessed saints, and to dispose ourselves as though we were to be taken out of this world and brought into the presence of the everlasting God. And since that bliss is yet deferred from us for a time, we may well think that as yet we are not ready nor worthy to come thereto and therefore we ought to prepare ourselves to be more ready another time. For blessed is that servant whom our Lord, when He shall come at the hour of death, shall find ready; for He shall take him and lift him up, high above all earthly things, into His everlasting joy and bliss.

CHAPTER XVIII

Of The Love Of Solitude And Silence

Seek for a convenient time to search your own conscience, and think often on the graciousness of God. Leave off all curious things and read such matters as shall stir you to compunction of heart for your sins, rather than to read only for occupying of the time. If you will withdraw yourself from superfluous words, and from unprofitable runnings-about, and from hearing of rumors and of vain tales, you shall find time convenient to be occupied in holy meditation.

The most holy men and women who ever were fled the company of worldly-living men, as far as they were able, and chose to serve God in the secret of their hearts; and one holy man said: 'As often as I have been among worldly company I have departed with less fervor of spirit than I had when I came.' And that we know well, whensoever we talk long, for it is not so hard always to keep silence as it is not to exceed in words when we speak much. It is also easier to be always solitary at home than to go forth into the world and not offend. Therefore he who intends to come to an inward setting of his heart in God and to have the grace of devotion must withdraw himself from the people. No man may safely appear among the people but he who would gladly be solitary if he might; no man is secure in authority, but he who would gladly be a subject; no one may firmly command but he who has learned gladly to obey; no one joys truly but he whose heart witnesses him to have a clean conscience; no one speaks surely but he who would gladly keep siilence if he might.

Always the surety of good men and of blessed men has been in meekness and in the dread of God; and though such blessed men shone in all virtue, yet they were not lifted up into pride therefor, but were the more diligent in the service of God and the more meek in all their doings. And contrarily, the surety of evil men rises from pride and presumption, and in the end deceives them.

Therefore, think yourself never sure in this life whether you are religious or secular; for oftentimes those who have been held in the sight of the people most perfect have been suffered to fall more grievously for their presumption. Also it is much more profitable to many persons that they sometimes have temptations than that they be always without them, lest perhaps they think themselves to be entirely secure, and be thereby lifted up into pride, or run to seeking of outward consolation.

O how pure a conscience should he have who would despise all transitory joy and would never meddle with worldly business. And what peace and inward quietness should he have who would cut away from himself all busyness of mind and only think on spiritual things.

No man is worthy to have spiritual comforts if he has not first been well exercised in holy compunction. And if you will have compunction, go into a secret place and put away from you all the clamorous noise of the world; for in your own cell you shall find great grace which you may easily lose without. Your own cell [or place of meditation] well lived in shall grow sweet and pleasant to you, and shall be to you thereafter a very dear friend; but if it is badly kept, it shall grow very tedious and irksome to you. If in the beginning you are often therein and keep it well in good prayers and in holy meditations, it shall afterwards be to you a singular friend and one of your most special comforts.

In silence and quietness of heart a devout soul profits much and learns the hidden secrets of scriptures, and finds there, also, many sweet tears in devotion, wherewith every night she washes herself from all sin, that she may be so much the more familiar with God as she is dissevered from the clamorous noise of worldly business. Therefore our Lord with His angels shall draw near to them and shall abide with them who for the love virtue withdraw themselves from their acquaintances and from their worldly friends. It is better that a man be solitary and well take heed of himself than that he do miracles in the world, forgetting himself. It is also a laudable thing in a religious person seldom to go forth, seldom to see others, and seldom to be seen by others.

Why will you see that which is not lawful for you to have? The world passes away with all its lusts and deceitful pleasures. Your sensual appetite moves you to go abroad but when the time is past, what do you bear home again but remorse of conscience and unquietness of heart? It is often seen that after a merry going-forth follows a sorrowful returning, and that a glad evening causes a heavy morning. And so all fleshly joy enters pleasantly, but in the end it bites and slays.

What may you see without your abode that you may not see within? Lo, within your own cell [or place of meditation] you may see heaven and earth, and all the elements whereof all earthly things are made! And what may you elsewhere see under the sun that may long endure? And if you might see all earthly things and also have all bodily pleasures present at once before you, what would it be but a vain sight? Lift up your eyes therefore to God in heaven, and pray heartily that you may have forgiveness for your offences.

Leave vain things to those who will be vain, and take heed only to those things that our Lord commands you. Shut fast the door of your soul, that is to say, your imagination, and keep it warily from the beholding of any bodily thing, as much as you may; and then lift up your mind to your Lord, open your heart faithfully to Him, and abide with Him in your own place, for you shall not find so much peace without.

If you had not gone forth so much as you have done, nor had given hearing to vain tales, you should have been in much more inward peace than you are. But since it delights you to hear new things, you shall therefore suffer sometimes both trouble of heart and unquietness of mind.

Chapter XIX

Of Compunction Of The Heart

If you will anything profit to the health of your soul, keep yourself always in the fear of God. Never desire to be fully at liberty, but keep yourself always under some wholesome discipline. Never give yourself to indiscreet mirth for any manner of thing, as much as your frailty may allow. Have perfect compunction and sorrow for your sins and you shall find thereby great inward devotion. Compunction opens to the sight of the soul many good things which levity of heart and vain mirth soon drive away. It is a marvel that any man can be merry in this life, if he consider well how far he is exiled out of his country and how great peril his soul daily stands in. But through inconstancy of heart and negligence of our faults we feel not, and we will not feel, the sorrow of our own soul, and oftentimes we laugh when we ought rather to mourn, for there is no perfect liberty nor true joy but in the dread of God and in a good conscience.

That person is very happy who has grace to avoid all things that hinder him from beholding his own sins and who can turn himself to God by inward compunction. And he is happy also who avoids all things that may offend or grieve his conscience. Fight strongly therefore against all sins, and do not fear overmuch because you are encumbered by an evil custom, for that evil custom may be overcome with a good custom. And do not offer as excuse that you are hindered by other men, for if you will leave your familiarity with others they will allow you to do your deeds without impediment.

Do not meddle with other men's goods nor busy yourself in great men's causes. Have always an eye to yourself, and diligently inform and admonish yourself before all others. If you have not the favor of worldly-living people, sorrow not therefor; but let it be your daily sorrow that you behave not yourself in your conversation as it behoves a good religious person to do. It is more expedient and more profitable that a man sometimes lack consolations in his life than that he have them always according to his will, especially fleshly consolations. Nevertheless, that we do not sometimes have heavenly comforts, or that we so seldom feel them, is through our own fault; for we seek not to have the true compunction of heart nor cast fully away from us the false outward comforts. Hold yourself therefore unworthy to have any consolation and worthy to have much tribulation.

When a man sorrows perfectly for his sins, then all worldly comforts are painful to him. A good man always finds matter enough why he ought rightfully to sorrow; for if he behold himself, or if he think of his neighbor, he sees well that no one lives here without great misery. And the more thoroughly that he considers himself, the more sorrow he has, for always the matter of true sorrow and of true inward compunction is the remembrance of our sins, wherewith we are so compassed on every side that seldom may we behold any spiritual things.

If we would more often think on our death than we do on long life, no doubt we should more fervently apply ourselves to amendment. But inasmuch as these things go not to the heart, and we yet love the flattering and false pleasures of this world, therefore we remain cold and void of devotion; and often it is through the weakness of the spirit that the wretched body so readily complains.

Pray therefore meekly to our Lord that He of His great goodness give you the spirit of compunction, and say with His devotees: 'Feed me, Lord, with the bread of compunction and give me to drink water of tears in great abundance.'

CHAPTER XX

Of Considering The Misery Of Mankind, and Wherein The Felicity Of Man Stands

A wretch you are, wheresoever you are and wheresoever you turn yourself, if you turn yourself not to God. Why are you so easily troubled when it falls not to you as you would and desire? What is he who has all things according to his will? Neither you nor I, nor any man living; for no one lives here without some trouble or anguish, though he may be a king or a pope.

Who do you think is in most favor wth God? Truly, he who gladly suffers most for God. But many persons weak and feeble in spirit say thus in their hearts: 'Lo, how good a life that man leads; how rich he is, how powerful he is, how high in authority, how great in sight of the people, and how fair and beauteous he is in appearance.' But if you take heed to the goodness everlasting, you shall well see that these worldly goods and worldly pleasures are worth but little, and that they are rather more grievous than pleasant; for they may not be had, nor kept, but by great labor and busyness of mind. The felicity of man stands not in abundance of worldly goods, but in abundance of spiritual goods, which are the gifts of God to a clean heart; and therefore moderation is best.

Truly, to live in this world is but misery; and the more spiritual that a man would be, the more painful it is to him to live, and the more plainly he feels the faults of man's corruption. For to eat, to drink, to sleep, to wake, to rest, to labor, and to serve all other necessities of the body, is great misery and great affliction to a devout soul, which would gladly be free from the bondage of sin so that it might without hindrance serve our Lord in purity of conscience and in cleanness of heart. The inward man is greatly grieved through bodily necessities in this world, wherefore all holy men desire that they might be delivered from such necessities.

But woe be to them who know not their own misery, and woe be to them who love this wretched and corruptible life! For some love it so much that if they might ever live here, though they might get their living but poorly with labor and begging, yet would they never care for the kingdom of God. O mad and unfaithful creatures are they who so deeply set their love in earthly things that they have no feeling nor taste but in fleshly pleasures. Truly, in the hour of death they shall know how vile and insignificant a thing it was that they so much loved. But holy saints and devout lovers of God heed not what pleases the flesh, nor what is pleasant in sight of the world. All their intent and desire they hold to things invisible, and fear lest by sight of things visible, they might be drawn down to the love of them.

My well-beloved brother, lose not the desire to profit in spiritual things, for you have yet good time and space. Why will you any longer defer the time? Arise, and now this same instant begin, and say thus: 'Now is the time to labor in good works; now is the time to fight in spiritual battle; and now is the time to make amends for mistakes of the past.' When you are troubled, then is the best time to merit and get rewards of God.

It behoves you to go through fire and water before you may come to the place of regeneration; and unless you can fully have the mastery over yourself you shall never overcome sin, nor live without great tediousness and sorrow. Wherefore we must hold ourselves in patience, and with good hope await the mercy of God till wretchedness is overpassed and this bodily life is changed into the life everlasting.

Oh how great is the frailty of man who is ever ready and prone to sin. This day you repent and tomorrow you fall again. Now you purpose to be wary and intend to go forth strongly in good works, and shortly after you do as though you never had taken such purpose. Rightfully therefore we ought to humble ourselves, and never to think any virtue or goodness is in us, we are so frail and so unstable. Soon may that be lost through negligence which with much labor and special grace was hardly gotten. Moreover, what shall become of us in the end, when we so soon grow dull and slow? Truly, sorrow and woe shall be to us if we fall to bodily rest now, as though we were in spiritual certainty, when there appears as yet neither sign nor token of virtue nor of good living in our conversation. Wherefore it would be expedient to us that we be yet again instructed as novices to learn good manners, if perchance by that means there could be found hereafter any trust of amendment and spiritual profit in our conversation.

Chapter XXI

Of The Remembrance Of Death

The hour of death will shortly come, and therefore take heed how you order yourself, for the common proverb is true: 'Today a man, tomorrow none.' And when you are out of sight you are quickly out of mind and soon shall you be forgotten.

O the great dullness and hardness of man's heart, that only thinks on things present, and little provides for the life to come! If you would do well, behave yourself in every deed and in every thought as though you should this instant die. If you had a good conscience you should not much fear death, and it would be better for you to leave sin than to fear death. O my dear brother, if you are not ready this day, how shall you be ready tomorrow? Tomorrow is a day uncertain, and you cannot tell whether you shall live so long.

What profit is it to us to live long when we thereby so little amend our life? Long life does not always bring us to amendment but oftentimes increases more sin. Would to God that we might be one day well conversant in this world. Many reckon their years of conversion, and yet there is but little fruit of amendment or of any good example seen in their conversation. If it is fearful to die, perhaps it is more perilous to live long. Blessed are those persons who ever have the hour of death before their eyes and who every day dispose themselves to die.

If you ever saw any man die, remember that you must go the same way. In the morning doubt whether you shall live till night, and at night think not yourself sure to live till the morrow. Be always ready, and live in such manner that death find you not unprepared. Remember how many have died suddenly and unprepared; for our Lord has called them in such hour as they least thought. And when that last hour shall come you shall begin to feel entirely otherwise of your life passed than you have done before; and you shall then sorrow greatly that you have been so slow and so negligent in the service of God as you have been. O how happy and wise is he, therefore, who labors now to stand in such a state in this life as he would be found in at his death. Truly, a perfect despising of the world and a fervent desire to profit in virtue, a love to be taught, a fruitful labor in works of penance, a ready will to obey, a full forsaking of ourselves, and a willing sufference of all adversities for the love of God, shall give us great trust that we shall die well.

O my dear brother, from how great peril and dread might you now deliver yourself, if you would always in this life dread to offend God and always have the coming of death suspect. Therefore study now to live so that at the hour of death you may rather joy than dread. Learn now to die to the world that you may then live in God. Learn also to despise all worldly things that you may then freely go to God. Chastise now your body with penance, that you may then have a sure and steadfast hope of salvation.

You are a fool if you think to live long, since you are not certain to live one day to the end. How many have been deceived through trust of long life and suddenly have been taken out of this world long before they had thought. How often have you heard it told that such a man was slain, and such a man was drowned, and such a man fell and broke his neck; this man as he ate his meat choked to death, and this man as he played took his death; one with fire, another with the sword, another with sickness, and some by theft, have suddenly perished. And so the end of all men is death, and the life of man, like a shadow, suddenly slides and passes away.

Think often who shall remember you after your death, and who shall pray for you; and do now for yourself all that you can, for you know not when you shall die or what shall follow after your death. While you have time, gather to yourself the riches immortal. Think abidingly on nothing but your soul's health. Set your study only on things that are of God and that belong to His honor. Make friends against that time by worshipping His saints and following their steps, so that when you shall go out of this world they may receive you into your everlasting home.

Keep yourself as a pilgrim and as a stranger here in this world, to whom nothing belongs of worldly business. Keep your heart free and always lifted up to God, for you have here no abiding home. Send your desires and your daily prayers always upward to God, and pray perseverantly that your soul at the hour of death may blessedly depart out of this world and go to God.

CHAPTER XXII

Of The Fervent Amending Of All Our Life, and That We Shall Especially Take Heed Of Our Own Soul's Health Before All Else

My son, be waking and diligent in the service of God, and think often why you are here and why you have forsaken the world. Was it not that you should live to God and be made a spiritual man? Yes, truly.

Therefore stir yourself to perfection; for in short time you shall receive the full reward of all your labors, and from thenceforth shall never come to you sorrow nor dread. Your labor shall be little and short, and you shall receive therefor again, everlasting rest and comfort. If you continue faithful and fervent in good deeds, without doubt our Lord will be faithful and liberal to you in His rewards. You shall always have a good trust that you shall come to the palm of victory; but you shall not set yourself in full certainty thereof, lest perhaps you grow dull and proud in heart.

A certain person who oftentimes doubted whether he was in the state of grace or not, once fell prostrate before God and said thus: 'O that I might know whether I shall persevere in virtue to the end of my life.' And immediately he heard inwardly in his soul the answer of our Lord, saying: 'What would you do if you knew you should persevere? Do now as you would do then, and you shall be safe.' And so immediately he was comforted and committed himself wholly to the will of God, and all his doubtfulness ceased, and never after would he curiously search to know what should become of him; but rather he studied to know what was the will of God concerning him, and how he might begin and end all his deeds that he should do, to the pleasure of God and to His honor.

One thing withdraws many from profiting in virtue and from amendment of life: that is, a horror and a false worldly dread that they may not endure the pain and labor that is needful for the getting thereof. But they shall most profit in virtue before all others who enforce themselves mightily to overcome those things that are most grievous and most contrarious to them. For a man profits there most, and there wins most grace, where he most overcomes himself and wherein he most mortifies his body to the soul.

But all men have not the same amount to mortify and overcome, for some have more passions than others have. Nevertheless a fervent lover of God, though he have greater passions than others, shall yet be stronger to profit in virtue than another who is better mannered and who has fewer passions, but is less fervent to virtue. Two things help a man much to amendment of life: that is, a mighty withdrawing of himself from those things that the body most inclines him to, and a fervent labor for such virtues as he has most need of.

Study also to overcome in yourself those things that in other men most offend you. And take always some special profit in every place, wherever you may be: if you see any good example, enforce yourself to follow it; and if you see any evil example, see that you avoid it. As your eye considers the works of others, just so and in the same way your works are considered by others.

O how joyous and how delectable it is to see religious men devout and fervent in the love of God, well mannered, and well taught in spiritual learning! And contrarily, how heavy and sorrowful it is to see them live inordinately, not using those things that they have chosen and taken themselves to. Also how ill-befitting a thing it is that a man be negligent in the purpose of his first calling and set his mind to things that are not committed to him.

A good religious man who is fervent in his religion takes all things well, and does gladly all that he is commanded to do. But a religious person who is negligent and slothful has trouble upon trouble and suffers great anguish and pain on every side; for he lacks the true inward comfort, and he is prohibited from seeking any outward comforts. Therefore a religious person who lives without discipline is apt to fall to great ruin. Also he who in religion seeks to have liberty and releasing of his duty shall always be in anguish and sorrow, for one thing or another shall ever displease him. Take heed how other religious persons do, who are very strictly kept under the rule of their religion. They go seldom forth, they live hardly, they eat poorly, and are clothed grossly; they labor much, speak little, watch long, rise early, make long prayers, read often, and keep themselves always in some wholesome discipline. Behold the monks and nuns of various Orders; how they rise every night to serve our Lord. And therefore it would be a great shame to you that you should grow slow and dull in so holy a work where so many laud and praise our Lord.

O how joyous a life would it be, if we should do nothing else but with heart and mouth continually praise our Lord. Now truly, if we should never need to eat, drink, nor sleep, but might always laud Him and only take heed to spiritual studies, then would we be much more happy and blessed than we are now, when we are bound of necessity to serve the body. O would to God that these bodily nourishings were turned into spiritual refections which, alas, we taste but seldom.

When a man comes to that perfection that he seeks not his consolation in any created thing, then begins God first to savor sweet unto him, and then he shall be content with everything that comes, whether it be pleasurable or irksome. And then he shall not be glad for any worldly profit, be it never so great, nor sorry for the wanting of it, for he has set himself and established himself wholly in God, who is to him all in all. For nothing perishes nor dies to God, but all things live to Him and serve Him without ceasing, after His bidding.

In everything remember the end, and that time lost cannot be called back again. Without labor and diligence you shall never get virtue. If you begin to be negligent, you begin to be feeble and weak. But if you apply yourself to fervor, you shall find great help of God; and for the love of virtue you shall find less pain in all your labors than you did first.

He who is fervent and loving is always quick and ready to all things that are of God and to His honor; and it is more labor to resist vices and passions than it is to strain and sweat in bodily labors. He who will not flee small sins shall little by little fall into greater, and you shall always be glad at night when you have spent the day before fruitfully.

Take heed of yourself, and stir yourself always to devotion; admonish yourself, and whatsoever you do for others forget not yourself. So much shall you profit in virtue as you can break your own will and follow the will of God.

– HERE ENDS THE FIRST BOOK –

BOOK TWO:

ADMONITIONS DRAWING TO THE INNER LIFE

Chapter I

Of Inward Conversation

He to whom all things are esteemed as they are and not as they are taken to be by worldly people is very wise and is rather taught by God than by man. And he who can inwardly lift his mind upward to God and can little regard outward things needs not to seek for time or place to go to prayers, or to do other good deeds or virtuous works. For the spiritual man may soon gather himself together and fix his mind in God because he never allows it to be fully occupied in outward things. Therefore his outward labors and his worldly occupations, necessary for the time, hinder him but little; for, as they come, so he applies himself to them and refers them always to the will of God. Moreover, a man who is well ordered in his soul heeds little the unkind demeanor of worldly people nor yet their proud behavior. As much as a man loves any worldly thing more than it should be beloved, so much his mind is hindered from the true ordinate love that he should have to God.

If you were well purged from all inordinate affections, then whatsoever befell to you should turn to your spiritual profit and the great increasing of grace and virtue in your soul. The cause why so many things displease you and trouble you, is that you are not yet perfectly dead to the world nor fully severed from the love of earthly things; and nothing so much defiles the soul as an impure love of creatures.

If you forsake to be comforted by worldly things, you may behold more perfectly the things of eternity, and you shall then sing continually lauds and praisings to God with great joy and inward gladness of heart.

CHAPTER II

Of A Meek Knowing Of Our Own Faults

Regard not much who is with you nor who is against you, but let this be your greatest study, that God may be with you in every thing that you do. Have a good conscience and He shall well defend you; and whomsoever He will help and defend, no malice may hinder nor grieve. If you can be still and suffer awhile, you shall without doubt see the help of God come in your need. He knows the time, place and means to deliver you, and therefore you must resign yourself wholly to Him. It pertains to Him to help and deliver you from all confusion.

Nevertheless it is oftentimes much profitable

to us for the more sure keeping of meekness that other men know our faults and reprove us of them. When a man humbles himself for his offences, he readily pleases others and reconciles himself to those whom he has offended. The humble man almighty God defends and comforts; to him He inclines Himself and sends him great plenty of His grace. To the humble man also He shows His secrets and lovingly He draws him to Himself; and after his oppression He lifts him up to glory. The humble man, when he has suffered confusion and reproof, is in good peace, for he trusts in God and not in the world. Moreover, if you will come to the highness of perfection, think not yourself to have anything profited in virtue till you can feel meekly in your heart that you have less humility and less virtue than any other man.

Chapter III

How Good It Is For A Man To Be Peaceful

First put yourself in peace, and then you may the better give peace to others. A peaceful and patient man profits more to himself and to others also than a man well-learned who is disquieted.

A man who is passionate oftentimes turns good into evil and readily believes the worse part, but a good peaceful man turns all things to the best and has suspicion toward no man.

He who is not content is often troubled with many suspicions, and neither is he quiet himself nor does he allow others to be quiet. He oftentimes speaks what he should not speak and he omits to speak what would be more expedient to say; he considers greatly what others are bound to do but to that which he is bound to himself he is fully negligent.

Therefore, have first a zeal and a respect to yourself and to your own soul, and then you may the more righteously and with the more due order of charity, have zeal toward your neighbor's. You are often ready to excuse your own faults, but you will not hear the excuses of your brethren. Truly, it would be more charitable and more profitable to you that you should accuse yourself and excuse your brother; for if you will be borne, you must also bear others. Behold how far you are yet from the perfect humility and charity of good religious souls, who cannot be angry with any but with themselves.

It is no great thing to be well conversant with good and gentle men, for that naturally pleases all people; and all men gladly have peace with them and most love them who are like themselves. But to live peaceably with evil men and with ill-tempered men who lack good manners and are untaught, and who are also contrarious unto us, is a great grace, and a manly deed and much to be praised; for it cannot be done except through great spiritual strength. Some persons can be quiet themselves and also can live quietly with others; and some cannot be quiet themselves, nor yet allow others to be quiet; they are grievous to others, but they are more grievous to themselves. And some can keep themselves in good peace and can also bring others to live in peace.

Nevertheless all our peace while we are in this mortal life stands more in meek suffering of troubles and of things that are contrarious unto us, than in not feeling them; for no man may live here without some trouble. Therefore he who can best suffer shall have most peace; and he is the very true vanquisher of himself, the lord of the world, and the true inheritor of the kingdom of God.

CHAPTER IV

Of A Pure Mind And A Simple Intent

Man is borne up from earthly things with two wings, that is to say, with simplicity and purity: simplicity is in the intent, and purity is in the love. The good, true, and simple intent looks towards God, but the pure love tastes His sweetness. If you are free from all inordinate love, no good deed shall hinder you, but you shall therewith increase in the way of perfection. If you intend well and seek nothing but God and the profit of your own soul and of your neighbor's, you shall have great inward liberty of mind. And if your heart is reconciled with God, then every creature shall be to you a mirror of life and a book of holy doctrine, for there is no creature so little nor so vile but that it shows and represents the goodness of God.

If you were inwardly in your soul pure and clean, you should then, without doubt, take all things to the best; for a pure heart transcends both heaven and hell. Such as a man is in his conscience inwardly, such he shows himself to be by his outward conversation. If there is any true joy in this world, it is had by a man of pure conscience; and if there is anywhere tribulation or anguish, an evil conscience knows it best. For, as iron put into the fire is cleansed from rust and is made entirely clean and pure, just so, a man turning himself wholly to God is purged from slothfulness and suddenly is changed into a new man.

When a man begins to grow dull and slow to spiritual endeavor, then a little labor greatly frightens him, and then he takes gladly outward comfort of the world and of the flesh; but when he begins perfectly to overcome himself and to walk strongly in the way of God, then he regards those labors as little that before he thought were very grievous and insupportable to him.

Chapter V

Of The Knowing Of Ourselves

We may not trust much in ourselves nor in our own wit, for oftentimes through our presumption we lack grace, and very little light of true understanding is in us. Many times what we have we lose through our negligence; and yet we see not, nor will we see, how blind we are. Oftentimes we do evil and in defence thereof we do much worse; and sometimes we are moved with passion and we think it is of a zeal to God. We immediately reprove small faults in our neighbors, but our own faults which are much greater we will not see. We feel often and ponder greatly what we suffer from others, but what others suffer from us we will not consider. He who would well and rightly judge his own faults should not so rigorously judge the faults of his neighbors.

A man who is inwardly turned to God takes heed of himself before all others, and he who can well take heed of himself can easily be still about other men's deeds. You shall never be a spiritual man and a devout lover of God unless you can keep yourself from meddling in other men's deeds and can especially take heed of your own. If you take heed wholly to God and to yourself, the faults that you see in others shall little move you.

Where are you when you are not present to yourself? And when you have run all about and have much considered other men's works, what have you profited thereby if you have forgotten yourself? If you will therefore have peace in your soul and be perfectly united to God in blessed love, set apart all other men's deeds and only set yourself and your own deeds before the eye of your soul; and if you see anything amiss in yourself, shortly reform it.

You shall much profit in grace if you keep yourself free from all temporal cares, and it shall hinder you greatly if you set value on any temporal things. Therefore let nothing be in your sight high, nothing great, nothing pleasing nor acceptable to you, unless it be purely God, or of God. Think all comforts vain that come to you by any creature. He who loves God, and his own soul for God, despises all other love; for he sees well that God alone, who is eternal and incomprehensible, and fulfills all things with His goodness, is the whole solace and comfort of the soul; and that He is the very true gladness of heart, and none other but only He.

Chapter VI

Of The Gladness Of A Good Conscience

The glory of a good man is the witness of God that he has a good conscience; have therefore a good conscience and you shall always have gladness. A good conscience may bear many wrongs and is ever merry and glad in adversities, but an evil conscience is always fearful and unquiet. Thus, you shall rest sweetly and blessedly if your own heart reprove you not.

Be never glad but when you have done well. Evil men never have perfect gladness nor feel inward peace, for there is no peace to wicked people. And though they say: 'We are in good peace; no evil shall come to us! Lo, who may grieve us or hurt us?' believe them not; for suddenly the wrath of God shall fall upon them, unless they amend, and all that they have done shall turn to nothing, and whatsoever they would have done shall be undone.

It is no grievous thing to a fervent lover of God to joy in tribulation, for all his joy and glory is in the Lord. It is a short glory that is given by man, and commonly some heaviness follows shortly after. The joy and gladness of good men is in God and of God, and their joy is in virtue and in a good life. He who desires the very perfect joy that is everlasting sets little value on temporal joy;

and he who seeks any worldly joy, or does not in his heart fully despise it, shows himself openly to love but little the joy of heaven.

He has great tranquility and peace of heart who regards neither praise nor censure, and he shall soon be pacified and content who has a good conscience. You are not the better because you are praised, nor the worse because you are criticised, for as you are, you are; and whatsoever is said of you, you are no better than almighty God, who is the searcher of man's heart, will witness you to be. If you behold well what you are inwardly, you shall not care much what the world speaks of you outwardly. Man sees the face but God beholds the heart; man beholds the deed but God beholds the intent of the deed. It is a great token of a meek heart, that a man ever shall do well and yet think himself to have done but little. And it is a great sign of purity of living and of an inward trust in God, when a man takes not his comfort of any creature. For he who has his mind always lifted up to God and is not bound with any inordinate affection outwardly, is in the degree and in the state of a holy and blessed man.

CHAPTER VII

Of The Visiting Of Grace

When the grace of God comes to a man, then he is made mighty and strong to do everything that belongs to virtue; and when grace withdraws, then he is made weak and feeble to do any good deed, and is, as it were, left only to pain and punishments. And if it happens so with you, yet despair not overmuch therefore and leave not your good deeds undone, but stand always strongly in obedience to the will of God, and turn all things that shall come to you to the laud and praising of His name. For after winter comes summer, and after the night comes the day, and after a great tempest shows again very clear and pleasant weather.

CHAPTER VIII

Of The Wanting Of All Solace And Comfort

It is no great thing to despise man's comfort when the comfort of God is present. But it is a great thing, and that a very great thing, that a man should be so strong in spirit that he may bear the wanting of them both; and for the love of God and to His honor should have a ready will to bear, as it were, a desolation of spirit, and yet in nothing to seek himself nor his own merits.

What proof of virtue is it, if a man is merry and devout in God when grace comes and visits the soul, for that hour is desired by every creature? He rides very safely whom the grace of God bears and supports; and what marvel is it, if he feels no burden who is borne up by Him who is almighty, and led by the sovereign guide who is God Himself? We are always glad to have solace and consolation; but we would have no tribulation, and we will not readily cast from us the false love of ourselves.

It behoves a man to fight long, and mightily to strive with himself, before he shall learn fully to overcome himself, and freely and readily set all his desires in God. When a man loves himself and much trusts to himself, he falls immediately to man's comforts. But the very true lover of God and the diligent follower of virtue falls not so easily to them; he seeks little such sensible sweetness and bodily delights, but rather is glad to suffer great hard labors and pain for the love of God.

Nevertheless, when spiritual comfort is sent to you of God, take it meekly and give thanks humbly for it. But know for certain that it is of the great goodness of God that it is sent to you, and not of your deserving. And see that you are not lifted up therefore unto pride, nor that you joy much thereof, nor presume vainly therein, but rather that you be the more meek for so noble a gift, and the more watchful and fearful in all your works; for that time will pass away, and the time of temptation will shortly follow after. When comfort is withdrawn, despair not therefore, but meekly and patiently await the visitation of God, for He is able and of sufficient power to give you more grace and more spiritual comfort than you had first.

Such alteration of grace is no new thing, and no strange thing to those who have had experience in the way of God; for in all great saints and in all lovers of God similar alteration has often been found. Wherefore the Psalmist, when he had abundance of spiritual comfort, said to our Lord that he trusted he should never be removed from such comfort. But after, when grace withdrew, he said: 'O Lord, Thou hast withdrawn Thy spiritual comforts from me and I am left in great trouble and heaviness.'

Yet nevertheless he despaired not therefor, but prayed heartily unto our Lord, and said: 'I shall busily cry to Thee, Lord, and I shall meekly pray to Thee for grace and comfort.' And immediately he had the effect of his prayer, as he witnesses himself, saying: 'Our Lord hath heard my prayer, and hath had mercy on me, and hath now again sent me His help and spiritual comfort.' And therefore he said afterwards: 'Lord, Thou hast turned my sorrow into joy, and Thou hast encompassed me with heavenly gladness.'

If almighty God has done thus with holy saints, it is not for us, weak and feeble persons, to despair, though we sometimes have fervor of spirit, and are sometimes left cold and void of devotion. The Spirit comes and goes according to His pleasure, and therefore Job said: 'Lord, Thou graciously visitest Thy lover in the morning, that is to say, in the time of comfort; and suddenly Thou provest him in withdrawing such comforts from him.'

Wherein then may I trust, or in whom may I have any confidence, but only in the great endless grace and mercy of God? For the company of good men and the fellowship of devout brethren and faithful friends, the having of holy books or of devout treatises, the hearing of sweet songs or of devout hymns, may little avail, and bring forth but little comfort to the soul when we are left to our own frailty and poverty. And when we are so left, there is no better remedy than patience, with a whole resigning of our own will to the will of God.

CHAPTER IX

Of Yielding Thanks To God For His Manifold Graces

Why do you seek rest here, since you are born to labor? Dispose yourself to patience rather than to comforts, to penance rather than to gladness. What temporal man would not gladly have spiritual comforts if he might always keep them? For spiritual comforts exceed by far all worldly delights and all bodily pleasures. All worldly delights are either foul or vain; but spiritual delights are only joyful and true, brought forth by virtues and sent by God into a pure soul. But such comforts no man may have whensoever he wishes, for the time of temptation follows swiftly after.

The false liberty of will and the inordinate trust that we have to ourselves is much contrary to the heavenly visitations. Our Lord does well in sending such comforts, but we do not well when we yield not all thanks therefor to Him again. The greatest cause why the gifts of grace may not readily come to us is that we are ungrateful to the Giver and yield not thanks to Him from whom all goodness comes. Grace is always given to them who are ready to yield thanks for it again, and therefore it is more likely given to the meek and taken from the proud.

I would have none of that consolation that should take from me compunction! And I would have none of that contemplation that should lift my soul into presumption! Every high thing in man's sight is not holy; every desire is not clean and pure; every sweet thing is not good; all that is dear to man is not always pleasant to God. We shall therefore gladly take such gifts as make us the more ready to forsake ourselves and our own will.

He who knows the comforts that come through the gift of grace and knows also how sharp and painful the absenting of grace is, shall not dare think that any goodness comes of himself; but he shall openly confess that of himself he is very poor and naked of all virtue. Yield therefore to God that which is His, and to yourself that which is your own; that is, thank God for His manifold graces and blame yourself for your offences. Hold in you always a sure foundation of meekness, and then the highness of virtue shall shortly be given unto you; for the high tower of virtue may not long stand unless it is borne up with the low foundation of meekness.

Those who are greatest in virtue are least in their own sight; and the more glorious they are, the meeker they are in themselves, full of truth and of heavenly joy, not desirous of any vainglory or praising of man. Also those who are fully established and confirmed in God may in no way be lifted up unto pride. They who ascribe all goodness to God seek no glory nor vain praisings in the world. They covet only to joy and to be glorified in God, and desire in heart that He may be honored, lauded, and praised, above all things, both in Himself and all His saints; and that is always the thing that perfect men most desire to bring about.

Be loving and thankful to God for the least benefit that He gives you, and then you shall be the better prepared and the more worthy to receive of Him greater benefits. Think the least gift that He gives is great; and the most despisable things take as special gifts and as great tokens of love. For if the greatness of the Giver is well considered, no gift that He gives shall seem little.

It is no little thing that is given by God, for though He send pain and sorrow, we should take them gladly and thankfully, since all that He allows to come unto us is for our spiritual health. If a man desire to hold the grace of God, let him be kind, and thankful for such grace as he has received, and patient when it is withdrawn; let him pray devoutly that it may shortly come again, and then let him be meek and humble in spirit, so that he lose it not through his presumption and pride of heart.

– HERE ENDS THE SECOND BOOK –

BOOK THREE:

THE INWARD
SPEAKING
OF GOD
TO A FAITHFUL
SOUL

CHAPTER I

That The Words Of God Are To Be Heard With Great Meekness, And That There Are But Few Who Ponder Them As They Ought To Do

'My son', saith our Lord, 'hear My words and follow them, for they are most sweet, far surpassing the wisdom and learning of all philosophers and of all the wise men of the world. My words are spiritual and cannot be fully comprehended by the wit of man. Neither are they to be turned and applied according to the vain pleasure of the hearer, but are to be heard in silence, with great meekness and reverence, with great inward affection of the heart, and in great rest and quietness of body and soul.'

O blessed is he, Lord, whom Thou informest and teachest, so that Thou mayst be merciful unto him, and so that he may not be left desolate and comfortless in his last days.

Then saith our Lord again: 'I have taught those who love Me since the beginning, and I still continue to speak to every creature. But many are deaf and will not hear, and many hear the world more gladly than Me, and more willingly follow the pleasures of the flesh than the pleasure of God.

'The world promises temporal things of small value and yet is served with great affection; but God promises high things and things eternal, and the hearts of the people are slow and dull. O who serves and obeys God in all things with so great a desire as he does the world, and as worldly authorities are served and obeyed? I think none. And why? For a little employment great journeys are taken, but for the life everlasting the people will scarcely lift their feet once from the ground. A thing that is of small price may be busily sought — sometimes for a penney men strive against one another; and for the promise of a little worldly profit men will strain and sweat both night and day.

'But alas for sorrow! For the everlasting prize, for the reward that may not be esteemed by man's heart, for the high honor and the glory that never shall have end, men are slow to take any manner of pain or labor. Be ashamed, you slow servant of God, that they are found more ready to works of death than you are to works of life, and that they joy more in vanity than you in truth. And yet they are often deceived by that which they have most trust in, but My promise deceives no man nor leaves any man who trusts in Me without some comfort. What I have promised I will perform, and what I have said, I will fulfill to every person, so that they abide faithfully in My love and dread unto the end; for I am the rewarder of all good men, and a strong prover of all devout souls.

'Write My words in your heart diligently, and often think upon them; for in time of temptation they shall be much necessary unto you. That which you understand not when you read it, you shall understand in the time of My visitation. I visit my servants two manner of ways; that is, with temptation, and with consolation. And two lessons daily I read unto them, one whereby I rebuke their vices, another whereby I stir them to increase in virtues. He who knows My words and despises them has that which shall judge him at the time of his death.'

O my Lord! Thou art all my riches; and all that I have, I have it from Thee. But what am I, Lord, that I dare thus speak to Thee? I am Thy poorest servant and a worm most abject; more poor, and more despisable than I can or dare say. Behold, Lord, that I am nothing, that I have nothing, and that of myself I am worth nothing. Thou only art good, righteous, and holy; Thou orderest all things, Thou givest all things, and Thou fulfillest all things with Thy goodness, leaving only the wretched sinner barren and void of heavenly comfort. Remember Thy mercies, and fill my heart with Thy manifold graces, for Thou wilt not that Thy works in me be made in vain. How may I bear the miseries of this life unless Thy grace and mercy do comfort me therein? Turn not Thy face from me; defer not Thy visiting of me: withdraw not Thy comforts from me, lest perhaps my soul become as dry earth without the water of grace, and become an unprofitable thing to Thee. Teach me, Lord, to fulfill Thy will and to live meekly and worthily before Thee, for Thou art all my wisdom and learning. Thou art He who knowest me as I am, and who knewest me before the world was made, and before I was born or brought into this life

CHAPTER II

That Grace Will Not Be Mixed With Love Of Worldly Things

'My son, grace is a precious thing and will not be mixed with any private love nor with worldly comforts. It behoves you to cast away all hindrances of grace if you will have the gracious gift thereof. Choose therefore a secret place and love to be alone, and keep yourself from hearing of vain tales and fables. Offer to God devout prayers and ask earnestly that you may have a contrite heart and a pure conscience. Think all the world is nothing, and prefer My service before all other things; for you may not have your mind on Me and therewithal delight in transitory pleasures. It behoves you, therefore, to withdraw yourself from your dearest friends, and from all your acquaintances, and to sequester your mind wholly from the inordinate desire of worldly comfort as much as you may.

'O how sure a trust shall it be to a man at his departing out of this world, to feel inwardly in his soul that no earthly love nor yet the affection of any passing or transitory thing has any rule in him! But a weak person, newly turned to God, may not so easily have his heart severed from earthly desires, and the worldly-living man knows not the freedom of a man who is inwardly turned to God. And therefore if a man will perfectly be spiritual and holy, he must as well renounce strangers as kinsfolk; and especially before all others he must be most wary of himself, for if he overcomes himself perfectly he shall the sooner overcome all other enemies. The most noble and most perfect victory is for a man to have the victory over himself. He, therefore, who holds himself so much subject that sensuality obeys to reason, and reason in all things is obedient to Me, is the true overcomer of himself and the lord of the world.

'But if you covet to come to that point, you must begin manfully, and set your axe to the root of the tree and fully cut away and destroy in yourself all the inordinate inclination that you have to yourself or to any private or material things. For of that vice, that a man loves himself inordinately, depends nearly all that ought summarily to be destroyed in man. And if that is truly overcome, immediately shall follow great tranquility and peace of conscience. But inasmuch as there are but few who labor to die to themselves, or to overcome themselves perfectly, therefore many lie still in their fleshly feelings and worldly comforts, and may in no way rise up in spirit above themselves; for it behoves him who will be free in heart and have contemplation of Me, to mortify all evil inclinations that he has to himself and to the world, and not to be bound to any creature by an inordinate or private love.'

CHAPTER III

How We Should Forget All Created Things In Order That We Might Find Our Creator

Lord, I have great need of Thy grace, and of Thy great singular grace, before I may come thither where no creature shall hinder me from the perfect beholding of Thee; for as long as any transitory thing holds me or has rule in me, I may not fly freely to Thee. He coveted to fly without hindrance who said: 'Who shall give me wings like a dove that I may fly into the bosom of my Lord!'

I see well that no man is more restful in this world than is that man who always has his mind and his whole intent upward to God, and nothing desires of the world. It behoves him therefore who would perfectly forsake himself and behold Thee, to rise above all creatures, and himself also, and through excess of mind to see and behold that Thou, maker of all things, hast nothing among all creatures like Thyself. Unless a man is clearly delivered from the love of all creatures, he may not fully tend to his creator, and that is the greatest cause why there are so few contemplatives; that is to say, because there are so few who will sequester themselves willingly from the love of created things.

For contemplation great grace is required, for it lifts up the soul and ravishes it up in Spirit above itself. And unless a man is lifted up in Spirit above himself and is clearly delivered in his love from all creatures and is perfectly and fully united to God, whatsoever he knows or whatsoever he has, either in virtue or learning, is worth but little before God. Therefore he shall have but little virtue and long shall he lie still in earthly pleasures, who accounts anything great or worthy to be praised but God alone; for all other things besides God are nothing, and are to be accounted as nothing. There is great difference between the wisdom of a devout man, enlightened by grace, and the learning of a subtle and studious scholar;

and that learning is much more noble and much more worthy that comes by the influence and gracious gift of God than that which is gotten by the labor and study of man.

Many desire to have the gift of contemplation, but they will not use such things as are required for contemplation. And one great hindrance of contemplation is that we stand so long in outward signs and in material things, and take no heed of the perfect mortifying of our body to the spirit. I know not how it is, nor with what spirit we are led, nor what we pretend, we who are called spiritual persons, that we take greater labor and study for transitory things than we do to know the inward state of our own soul.

But alas for sorrow, as soon as we have made a little recollection to God, we run forth to outward things and do not search our own conscience with due examination, as we should, nor heed where our affection rests, nor sorrow that our deeds are so evil and so unclean as they are. In ancient times, the people corrupted themselves with fleshly uncleanness, and therefore followed the great flood; and truly, when our inward affection is corrupted, our deeds following thereon are also corrupted, for of a clean heart springs the fruit of a good life.

It is oftentimes asked what deeds such a man has done, but of what zeal or with what intent he did them is little regarded. Whether a man is rich, strong, fair, able, a good writer, a good singer, or a good laborer, is often inquired; but how poor he is in spirit, how patient and meek, how devout, and how inwardly turned to God, is little regarded. Nature beholds the outward deed, but grace turns her to the inward intent of the deed. The first is often deceived, but the second puts her trust wholly in God and is not deceived.

Chapter IV

Of The Differences Between Nature And Grace

'My son, take good heed of the motions of nature and grace for they are very subtle and much contrary, the one to the other, and hardly may they be known asunder, unless it is by a spiritual man who is inwardly illumined in his soul through grace. Every man desires some goodness and pretends somewhat of goodness in all his words and deeds, and therefore under pretence of goodness many are deceived.

'Nature is wily and full of deceit, and draws many to her whom she oftentimes snares and deceives; and ever she beholds her own wealth as the goal of her work. But grace walks simply without deceit, she declines from all evil, she pretends no guile, but all things she does purely for God, in whom finally she rests.

'Nature will not gladly die, nor gladly be oppressed or overcome; neither will she be gladly under another nor be kept in subjection. But grace studies how she may be mortified to the world, and to the flesh; she resists sensuality, she seeks to be subject, she desires to be overcome, she will not use her own liberty. She loves to be held under holy discipline, and covets not to have lordship over any one creature but to live and to stand always under the fear of God, and for His love is always ready to bow herself meekly under every creature.

'Nature labors for her own profit and advantage, and much beholds what winning comes to her by others. Grace beholds not what is profitable to herself, but what is profitable to many. Nature gladly receives honor and reverence, but grace refers all honor and reverence to God. Nature dreads reprovings and despisings; but grace joys, for the name of God, to suffer them both and takes them, when they come, as special gifts of God. Nature loves idleness and bodily rest; but grace cannot be idle without doing some good deed, and therefore she seeks gladly some profitable labors.

'Nature desires fair and curious things. But grace delights in meek and simple things; she despises not hard things, nor refuses to be clad in poor clothing and simple garments. Nature gladly beholds things temporal, she joys at worldly winnings, is heavy for worldly losses, and is quickly moved by a sharp word. But grace beholds things everlasting. She trusts not in things temporal, and is not troubled with the loss of them, nor grieved by an angry word; for she has laid her treasure in God and in spiritual things, which may not perish. Nature is covetous and more gladly takes than gives; she loves much to have property and private things. But grace is piteous and liberal to the poor, she flees singular profit, she is content with little and judges it more blessed to give than to take.

'Nature inclines to the love of creatures, to the love of the flesh, to vanities and runnings-about, and to see new things in the world. But grace draws a man to the love of God and to the love of virtues; she renounces all created things, she flees the world, she hates desires of the flesh, she restrains liberty and wandering-about, and avoids as much as she may to be seen among gatherings of people. Nature gladly has some outward solace wherein she may delight in her outward senses. but grace seeks only to be comforted in God and to delight her in His goodness above all things.

'Nature does all things for her own winning and singular profit; she may do nothing free, but hopes always to have the same back again, or more, or applause, or favor of the people; and covets much that her deeds and works be greatly pondered and praised. But grace seeks no temporal thing, and no other reward for her hire but only God. She will have no more of temporal goods than shall be needful for the getting of the goods everlasting, and cares not for the vain praise of the world.

'Nature joys greatly in many friends and kinsfolk, and glories much in a noble place of birth and in her noble blood and kindred; she joys with mighty men, she flatters rich men, and is merry with those who she thinks similar to her in nobleness of the world. But grace makes a man to love his enemies, she has no pride in worldly friends; she regards not the nobleness of kin, nor the house of her father, unless the more virtue is there. She favors more the poor than the rich, she has more compassion for an innocent than for a mighty man; she joys ever in truth and not in falsehood, and always comforts good men more and more to profit and grow in virtue and goodness, and to seek daily more high gifts of grace, that they may through good virtuous works be made into the sons of God.

'Nature immediately complains for the wanting of a very little thing that she would have or for a little worldly sorrow. But grace bears gladly all neediness and wantings of the world. Nature inclines all things to herself and to her own profit as much as she may; she argues for herself, and strives and fights for herself. But grace renders all things to God, of whom all things flow and spring originally; she ascribes no goodness to herself and presumes not of herself; she strives not and prefers not her own opinion before other men's, but in every sentence she submits her meekly to the eternal wisdom and judgement of God.

'Nature covets to know and to hear new secret things. She will that her works be showed outwardly, and will have experience of many things in the world by her outward senses; she desires also to be known and to do great things in the world, whereof applause and praising may follow. But grace cares not for any new things nor for any curious things, whatsoever they may be; for she knows well that all such things come of vanity, and that no new things may long endure upon earth.

'She teaches to restrain the outward senses and to avoid all vain pleasure and outward show, and meekly keeps secret things that in the world would be greatly marvelled at and praised. And in everything and in every science she seeks some spiritual profit to herself, and praise and honor to almighty God. She will not that her good deeds nor her inward devotion be outwardly known, but most desires that our Lord be blessed in all His works, who gives all things freely of His great and excellent love.

'This grace is a light from heaven and a spiritual gift of God. It is the proper mark and token of elect people and a guarantee of the everlasting life. It lifts a man from love of earthly things to the love of heavenly things, and makes a carnal man to be a man of God. And the more that nature is oppressed and overcome, the more grace is given, and the soul through new gracious visitations is daily shaped anew and formed more and more to the image of God.'

CHAPTER V

Of The Corruption Of Nature And Of The Worthiness Of Grace

O Lord God, who hast made me to Thine image and likeness, grant me this grace that Thou hast shown to be so great and so necessary to the health of my soul, that I may overcome this wretched nature which draws me always to sin and to the losing of my own soul. I feel in my flesh the law of sin fighting strongly against the law of my spirit, which leads me as a slave to obey my sensuality in many things; nor may I resist the passions thereof unless Thy grace doth assist me.

I have therefore great need of Thy grace, and a great abundance of it, if I shall overcome this wretched nature which always from my youth has been ready and prone to sin. In my inward self, that is, in the reason of my soul, I delight myself in Thy laws and in Thy teachings, knowing that they are good, righteous and holy; and that all sin is evil, and to be fled and avoided. Yet in my outward self, that is to say, in my fleshly feeling, I serve the law of sin when I obey my sensuality rather than my reason. And of this it follows also that I will good, but I may not for weakness perform it without Thy grace. And sometimes I intend to do many good deeds but, because the grace that should help me is lacking, I go backward and fail in my doing. I know the way to perfection, and I see clearly how I should do; but I am so oppressed with the heavy burden of this corrupt body of sin, that I lie still and rise not to perfection. O Lord, how necessary therefore is Thy grace to me, to begin well, to continue well, and to end well; for without Thee I may do nothing that is good.

O heavenly grace, without which our merits are worth nothing, and the gifts of nature to be considered nothing; and beauty, strength, wit, and eloquence may avail nothing! Come Thou, shortly, and help me! The gifts of nature are common to good men and to bad; but grace and love are the gifts of elect and chosen people, whereby they are marked, and made able and worthy to reach the kingdom of God. This grace is of such worthiness that neither the gift of prophecy, nor the working of miracles, nor the gift of wisdom and knowledge, may avail anything without it; nor yet may faith, hope, or other virtues, be acceptable to Thee without grace and love.

O blessed grace, that maketh the poor in spirit to be rich in virtue and him who is rich in worldly goods to be meek and low in heart! Come and descend into my soul, and fulfill me with Thy spiritual comforts, so that I do not fail and faint for weariness and dryness!

I beseech Thee, Lord, that I may find grace in Thy sight, for Thy grace shall suffice to me; though I am tempted and vexed with troubles on every side, yet I shall not need to fear while Thy grace is with me. For she is my strength, she is my comfort, my counsel and help. She is stronger than all my enemies and wiser than all the wisest of this world. She is the mistress of truth, the teacher of discipline, the light of the heart. She is the comfort of trouble, the driver-away of heaviness, the avoider of dread, the nourisher of devotion, and the bringer-in of sweet tears and devout weepings. What am I then, without grace, but a dry stock to cast away! Grant me, therefore, that Thy grace may prevent me and follow me, and make me ever busy and diligent in good works unto my death. So may it be!

CHAPTER VI

That It Is Sweet And Delectable To Serve God, And To Forsake The World

Now shall I speak yet again to Thee, my Lord, and not cease. And I shall say in the ears of my Lord: My God and King who is in heaven! O how great is the abundance of Thy sweetness which Thou hast hidden and kept for those who dread Thee! But what is it then to those who love Thee? Truly, it is the unspeakable sweetness of contemplation that Thou givest to those who love Thee. In this, Lord, Thou hast most showed the sweetness of Thy love to me, that when I was not, Thou madest me; and when I wandered far from Thee Thou broughtest me again to serve Thee, and commandest me to love Thee.

O fountain of love everlasting, what shall I say of Thee! How may I forget Thee who hast promised thus lovingly to remember me! When I was about to perish, Thou has shown Thy mercy to me above all that I could have thought or desired, and hast sent me of Thy grace and of Thy love above my merits. But what shall I give to Thee again for all this goodness? It is not given to all men to forsake the world and to take a solitary life and only to serve Thee. And yet it is no great burden to serve Thee, whom every creature is bound to serve. It ought not therefore to seem any great thing to me to serve Thee, but rather it should seem a great wonder to me that Thou wilt receive so poor and so unworthy a creature as I am into thy service, and that Thou wilt join me to Thy well-beloved servants.

Lo, Lord, all things that I have and all that I do Thee service with is Thine. And yet Thy goodness is such that Thou rather servest me than I Thee. For behold, heaven and earth and the planets and stars, which Thou hast created to serve man are ready at thy bidding, and do daily that which Thou hast commanded. And Thou hast also ordained angels to the ministry of man. But above all this, Thou hast promised to serve man Thyself and hast promised to give Thyself unto him.

What then shall I give to Thee in return for this thousand-fold goodness? Would to God that I might serve Thee all the days of my life, or at the least that I might one day be able to do Thee faithful service; for Thou art worthy all honor, service, and praising, forever. Thou art my Lord and my God, and I Thy poorest servant, most bound before all others to love and praise Thee; and I never ought to grow weary of the praising of Thee. This is what I ask and desire, that I may always laud Thee and praise Thee. Promise therefore, most merciful Lord, to supply whatsoever is lacking in me; for it is great honor to serve Thee, and for Thy love to despise all earthly things.

They shall have great grace who freely submit themselves to Thy holy service. And they shall find also the most sweet consolation of the Spirit and shall have great freedom of spirit here who forsake all worldly business and choose a hard and strict life in this world for Thy name.

O glad and joyful service of God, by which a man is made free and holy, and blessed in the sight of God! O holy state of religion, which makes a man similar to the angels, pleasing to God, dreadful to wicked spirits, and to all faithful people very highly commendable! O service much to be embraced and always to be desired, by which the high goodness is won, and the everlasting joy and gladness is gotten without end!

CHAPTER VII

Of The Marvellous Effect Of The Love Of God

O my Lord God, most faithful lover, when Thou comest into my heart, all that is within me doth joy! Thou art my glory and the joy of my heart, my hope and my whole refuge in all my troubles. But inasmuch as I am yet feeble in love and imperfect in virtue, therefore I have need to have more comfort and more help from Thee.

Consent, therefore, oftentimes to visit me and to instruct me with Thy holy teachings. Deliver me from all evil passions and heal my sick heart from all earthly pleasure, that I may be inwardly healed and purged from all inordinate affections and vices, and be made ready and able to love Thee, strong to suffer for Thee, and stable to persevere in Thee.

Love is a great and goodly thing, and alone makes heavy burdens light, and bears in the same balance things pleasing and displeasing. It bears a heavy burden and feels it not, and makes bitter things to be savory and sweet. The noble love of God perfectly printed in man's soul makes a man to do great things and stirs him always to desire perfection and to grow more and more in grace and goodness.

Love will always have his mind upward to God and will not be occupied with things of the world. Love will also be free from all worldly affections, that the inward sight of the soul may not be darkened or lost, and that his affection to heavenly things may not be diminished by an inordinate winning or losing of worldly things. Nothing, therefore, is sweeter than love, nothing higher, nothing stronger, nothing greater, nothing more joyful, nothing fuller, and nothing better in heaven nor in earth; for love descends from God and may not rest finally in anything lower than God. Such a lover flies high, he runs swiftly, he is merry in God, he is free in soul, he gives all for all and has all for all; for he rests in one high goodness above all things, of whom all goodness flows and proceeds. He beholds not only the gift, but the Giver, above all gifts.

Love knows no measure but is fervent without measure. It feels no burden; it regards no labor; it desires more than it may attain; it complains of no impossibility, for it thinks all things that may be done for his beloved possible and lawful unto him. Love therefore does many great things and brings them to fruition, wherein he who is no lover faints and fails.

Love wakes much and sleeps little, and sleeping, sleeps not. It faints and is not weary, is restrained of liberty and is in great freedom. It sees causes of fear and fears not; but as a burning ember or spark of fire, flames always upward by fervor of love unto God, and through the special help of grace is delivered from all perils and dangers.

He who is thus a spiritual lover knows well what his voice means which says: 'Thou, Lord God, art my whole love and my desire! Thou art all mine and I all Thine! Spread my heart into Thy love that I may know how sweet it is to serve Thee, and how joyful it is to laud Thee, and to be as though I were entirely melted into thy love.' O I am immersed in love and go far above myself for the great fervor that I feel of Thy unspeakable goodness! I shall sing to Thee the song of love; and my soul shall never be weary to praise Thee with the joyful song of love that I shall sing to Thee. I shall love Thee more than myself, and not myself but for Thee. And I shall love all others in Thee and for Thee, as the law of love commands which is given by Thee.

Love is swift, pure, meek, joyous and glad, strong, patient, faithful, wise, forbearing, manly, and never seeking himself nor his own will; for whensoever a man seeks himself, he falls from love. Love is circumspect, meek, righteous, not weak, not frivolous nor heeding vain things; sober, chaste, stable, quiet and well restrained in his outward senses. Love is subject and obedient to his superior, vile and despisable in his own sight, devout and thankful to God; trusting and always hoping in Him, and that even when he has but little devotion or little savor in him, for without some sorrow or pain no man may live in love.

He who is not always ready to suffer, and to stand fully at the will of his beloved, is not worthy to be called a lover; for it behoves a lover to suffer gladly all hard and bitter things for his beloved and not to decline from his love for any contrarious thing that may befall unto him.

Chapter VIII

How Grace Is To Be Kept Close Through The Virtue Of Meekness

'My son, it is much more expedient, and the surer way for you, that you hide the grace of devotion, and speak not much of it nor much regard it, but despise yourself the more for it, and think yourself unworthy any such gracious gift of God. And it is not good to cleave much to such affections as may be soon turned into the contrary. When you have the grace of devotion, consider how wretched and how needy you were when you had no such grace. The profit and increase of spiritual life is not only when you have devotion, but rather when you can meekly and patiently bear the withdrawing and the absence thereof; and yet cease not your prayers nor leave your other good deeds that you are accustomed to do, undone; but to your power, and as far as you are able, to do your best therein and forget not your duty, and be not negligent because of any dullness or unquietness of mind which you feel.

'Nevertheless there are many persons who, when any adversity falls to them, are immediately impatient, and are made thereby very slow and dull to do any good deed, and hinder themselves greatly. For the way that he shall take is not in the power of man; but it is in the grace of God only, to dispose according to His will, and to whom He will, as it shall please Him, and not otherwise. Some unaware persons, through an indiscreet desire that they have had to obtain the grace of devotion, have destroyed themselves; for they wished to do more than was in their power to do. They would not acknowledge the measure of their gift nor the littleness of their own strength; but would rather follow the pride of their heart than the judgement of reason. And because they presumed to do greater things than were pleasing to God, therefore they lost suddenly the grace that they had before. They were left needy and without comfort, who thought to build their nests in heaven, and so they were taught not to presume of themselves, but meekly to trust in God and in His goodness.

'Such persons also who are beginners and yet lack experience in spiritual travail may easily err and be deceived unless they will be ruled by counsel of others; and if they must necessarily follow their own counsel and in no way be removed therefrom, it will be very perilous to them in the end. It is not often seen that those who are wise and learned in their own sight will be meekly ruled or ordered by others. Therefore it is better to have little learning with meekness, than great learning with vain pleasure therein; and it is better to have little learning with grace, than much learning whereof you should be proud.

'He does not discreetly who in time of devotion sets himself entirely to spiritual mirth and, as it were, to a heavenly gladness, forgetting his former desolation and the meek dread of God. Neither does he well nor virtuously who in time of trouble or of any manner of adversity or gravity, bears himself exceedingly desperately, and feels not and thinks not so trustfully of Me as he ought. He who in time of peace and of spiritual comfort thinks himself overly secure, shall commonly be found, in time of battle and of temptation, overly dejected and fearful. But if you could always remain meek and little in your own sight, and could order well the motions of your own soul, you should not so soon fall into presumption or into despair, nor so readily offend almighty God. Wherefore, this is good and wholesome counsel: that when you have the spirit of fervor, you think how you shall do when fervor is past; and when it happens so with you, you think that fervor may soon come again, which to My honor and to your proving I have withdrawn for a time. And it is more profitable to you that you should be so proved, than that you should always have prosperous things according to your own will.

'Merits are not to be thought great in any person because he has many visions or many spiritual comforts, nor because he has clear understanding of scriptures, or is set in a high position. But if he is stably grounded in meekness, and is filled with love; if he seeks wholly the worship of God, and in nothing regards himself; if fully in his heart he can despise himself, and also covet to be despised of others, then may he have good trust that he has somewhat profited in grace and that he shall in the end have great reward of God for his good travail.'

CHAPTER IX

That The Very True Solace And Comfort Is In God

Whatsoever I may desire or think to my comfort, I look for it not here, but I trust to have it in Thee. For if I alone might have all the solace and comfort of this world, and might use the delights thereof according to my own desire without sin, it is certain that they might not long endure. Wherefore my soul may not fully be comforted nor perfectly be refreshed but in God only, who is the Comforter of the poor in spirit, and the Embracer of the meek and low in heart. Await, my soul, await the promise of God, and you shall have the abundance of all goodness in Him. If you inordinately covet these goods present, you shall lose the goodness eternal. Have therefore goods present in use and goodness eternal in desire.

You may in no manner be satisfied with temporal goods, for you are not created to rest yourself in them. For if you alone might have all the goods that ever were created and made, you might not therefore be happy and blessed; but your blessedness and your full felicity stands only in God who has made all things. And that is not such felicity as is commended by the foolish lovers of the world, but such as good men and women hope to have in the bliss of God, and as some spiritual persons, clean and pure in heart, sometimes do taste here in this present life, whose conversation is in heaven. All worldly solace and all man's comfort is vain and short, but that comfort is blessed and reliable that is perceived by the soul inwardly in the heart.

A devout follower of God bears always about with him his Comforter and says thus unto Him: 'My Lord, I beseech Thee that Thou be with me in every place and every time, and that it be to me a special solace, gladly for Thy love to want all man's solace. And if Thy solace is lacking also, grant that Thy will and Thy right proving of me may be to me a singular comfort and a high solace. Thou shalt not always be angry with me, nor shalt Thou threaten me forever. So may it be.

CHAPTER X

That All Our Study And Busyness Of Mind Ought To Be Put In God

'My son', saith our Lord to His servant, 'allow Me to do with you what I will, for I know what is best and most expedient for you. You work in many things according to your human reason and as your affection and your worldly policy stirs you, and so you may easily err and be deceived.'

O Lord, it is true, all that Thou sayest. Thy providence is much better for me than all that I can do or say for myself. Wherefore it may well be said and verified that he stands very uncertainly who sets not all his trust in Thee. Therefore, Lord, while my wits abide steadfast and stable, do with me in all things as it pleaseth Thee, for it may not be but well, all that Thou dost. If Thou wilt that I be in light, bless Thee; and if Thou wilt I be in darkness, bless Thee. If Thou wouldst comfort me, bless Thee; and if Thou wilt I live in trouble and without all comfort, bless Thee in equal measure.

'My son, so it behoves you to be. If you will walk with Me, as ready must you be to suffer as to joy, and as gladly be needy and poor as wealthy and rich.'

Lord, I will gladly suffer for Thee whatsoever Thou wilt shall fall upon me. With the same thanks will I take of Thy hand good and bad, bitter and sweet, gladness and sorrow; and for all things that shall befall to me, heartily will I thank Thee. Keep me from sin, Lord, and I shall dread neither death nor hell. Put not my name out of the book of life, and it shall not grieve me, whatsoever troubles befall me.

CHAPTER XI

How A Man Should Order Himself In His Desires

'My son', saith our Lord, 'in everything that you desire, you should say: "Lord, if it be Thy will, let it be done as I ask; and if it be to Thy praising, let it be fulfilled in Thy name. And if Thou regard it as good and profitable to me, give me grace to use it to Thine honor. But if Thou know it hurtful to me and not profitable to the health of my soul, then take from me such desire."

'Every desire comes not of the Spirit though it seem right and good, for it is sometimes very difficult to judge whether a good or an evil thought moves you to this thing or to that; or whether you are moved by My will. Many are deceived in the end, who first seemed to have been moved by My Spirit.

'Therefore, you should desire and ask whatsoever comes to your mind with a fear of God and with meekness of heart; and with a whole forsaking of yourself, you should commit all things to God and say thus: "Lord, Thou knowest what thing is to me most profitable; do this or that according to Thy will. Give me what Thou wilt, as much as Thou wilt, and when Thou wilt. Do with me as Thou knowest best to be done, as it shall please Thee, and as it shall be most to Thine honor. Put me where Thou wilt, and freely do with me in all things according to Thy will. I am Thy creature and I am in Thy hands; lead me, and turn me where Thou wilt. Lo, I am Thy servant, ready to all things that Thou commandest, for I desire not to live to myself, but to Thee. Would to God it might be worthily and profitably to Thine honor!"'

Most benign Lord, grant me Thy grace, that it may always be with me, and work with me and persevere with me unto the end. Grant that I may ever desire and will that which is most pleasing and most acceptable to Thee. Let thy will be my will, and let my will always follow Thy will and best accord therewith. Let there always be in me one will and one desire with Thee, and grant that I have no power to will or not to will, but as Thou wilt or will not. Grant me that I may die to all things that are in the world, and that for Thee I may love to be despised and to be as a man unknown in this world. Grant me also, above all things that can be desired, that I may rest in Thee, and fully in Thee pacify my heart. For Thou, Lord, art the very true peace of heart and the perfect rest of body and of soul, and without Thee all things are grievous and unquiet. Wherefore, in that peace which is in Thee, one high, one blessed, and one endless goodness, shall I always rest me. So may it be.

CHAPTER XII

How Our Lord God Savors To His Lover Sweetly Above All Things And In All Things

Our Lord God is to me all in all! And since He is so, what would I more have, or what can I more desire? O this is a savory and sweet word, to say that our Lord is to me all in all; but that is to him who loves the Lord and not the world.

To him who understands is said enough, but yet to repeat it often is pleasing to him who loves. I may therefore more plainly speak of this matter and say: Lord, when Thou art present to me all things are pleasant and agreeable, but when Thou art absent all things are grievous and despisable. When Thou comest, Thou makest my heart restful and bringest into it a new joy; Thou makest Thy lover to feel and understand the truth, and to have a true judgement in all things and in all things to laud Thee and praise Thee. O Lord, without Thee nothing may long be agreeable nor pleasant, for if anything is to be pleasant and savory it must be through help of Thy grace and be seasoned with the spicery of Thy wisdom.

To him to whom Thou savorest well, what shall not savor well? And to him whom Thou savorest not well unto, what may be joyful or pleasing? Worldly-wise men and they who savor earthly delights fail of this wisdom, for in worldly wisdom is found great vanity, and in fleshly pleasures is only death. Therefore they who follow Thee, Lord, by despising of the world and by perfect mortifying of their fleshly lusts, are known to be very wise; for they are led from vanity to truth, and from fleshly pleasures to spiritual purity. To such persons God savors wondrously sweet. And whatsoever they find in created things, they refer it all to the laud and to the praising of their creator; for they see well that there is great difference between the creature and the creator, between time and eternity, and between the created and the uncreated light.

O everlasting light, far passing all things that are made, send down the beams of Thy light from above, and purify, gladden, and illumine in me all the inward parts of my heart! Quicken my spirit with all the powers thereof, that it may cleave fast and be joined to Thee in joyful gladness of spiritual ravishings. O when shall that blessed hour come that Thou shalt visit me and gladden me with Thy blessed presence, so that Thou art to me all in all? As long as that gift is not given to me, there shall be in me no full joy.

But alas for sorrow! My old nature, that is, my earthly affection, still lives in me and is not yet fully mortified and perfectly dead in me. For yet strives the flesh strongly against the spirit, and moves great inward battle against me, and suffers not the kingdom of my soul to live in peace.

But Thou, good Lord, who hast the lordship over all the power of the sea and dost assuage the streams which from it flow, arise and help me! Break down the power of mine enemies which always move this battle in me! Show the strength of Thy goodness, and let the power of Thy right hand be glorified in me! For there is to me no other hope nor refuge but in Thee only, my Lord, my God! to whom be joy, honor and glory everlastingly.

CHAPTER XIII

Of The Acknowledging Of Our Own Infirmities And Of The Miseries Of This Life

I shall acknowledge against myself all my unrighteousness, and I shall confess to Thee, Lord, all the unstableness of my heart. Oftentimes it is but a little thing that casts me down and makes me dull and slow to all good works. Sometimes I intend to stand strongly, but when a little temptation comes, it is to me a great anguish and grief. Sometimes of a very little thing a grievous temptation rises, and when I think myself to be somewhat secure and imagine that I have the upper hand, suddenly I feel myself all but overcome by a light temptation.

Behold, therefore, good Lord, behold my weakness and my frailness, best known to Thee above all others! Have mercy on me, Lord, and deliver me from the filthy bogs of sin, that my feet never become fixed in them. But it often grudges me sorely and confounds me before Thee, that I am so unstable and so weak, so frail to resist my passions. And though they draw me not always to consent, yet nevertheless their cruel assaults are very grievous to me, so that it is tedious to me to live in such warfare. But yet such battle is not entirely unprofitable to me, because thereby I know the better my own infirmities, for I see well that such wicked fantasies do rise in me much sooner than they go away.

But would to God that Thou, most mighty God, lover of all faithful souls, wouldst consent to behold the labor and the sorrow of me, Thy poorest servant, and that Thou wouldst assist me in all things that I have to do! Strengthen me, Lord, with heavenly strength, so that neither my own inherent inclinations nor my wretched flesh, which is not yet fully subject to the spirit, have power or lordship over me!

But alas, what life is this, where no trouble nor misery is lacking, where every place is full of snares and of mortal enemies! For while one trouble or temptation is going away, another comes; and while the first conflict is yet enduring, many others sudenly arise, more than can be thought. How may this life therefore be loved that has such bitterness and that is subject to so many miseries? And how may it be called a life that brings forth so many deaths and so many spiritual plagues? And yet it is beloved and much delighted in by many persons. The world is often reproved that it is deceitful and vain, and yet it is not easily forsaken, especially when the lusts of the flesh are allowed to have rule. Some things stir a man to love the world and some to despise it. The lust of the flesh, the lust of the eye, and the pride of the heart, stir man to love the world. But the pains and miseries that follow them cause hatred and tediousness of it again.

But alas for sorrow, a little delectation overcomes the mind of those who are much inclined to love the world, and drives out of their hearts all heavenly desire, insomuch that many account it as a joy of paradise to live under such sensual pleasures, and that is because they neither have seen nor tasted the sweetness in God, nor the inward gladness that comes of virtues. But they who perfectly despise the world and who study to live under holy discipline, are not ignorant of the heavenly sweetness that is promised to spiritual men, and they see also how grievously the world errs and how grievously it is deceived in diverse ways.

CHAPTER XIV

That Men Are Not Always To Be Believed

Lord, send me help in my troubles, for man's help is worth little! How often have I not found friendship where I thought I should find it; and how often have I found it where I least presumed it to be. Wherefore it is a vain thing to trust in man, for the real trust and health of righteous men is only in Thee. Therefore, blessed art Thou, Lord, in all things that happen to us; for we are weak and unstable, soon deceived, and soon changed from one thing to another.

Who may so warily and so assuredly keep himself in everything, that he shall not sometimes fall into some deceit or into some perplexity? Truly, very few. But he who trusts in Thee and who seeks Thee with a pure heart slides not so often from Thee. And if it happen that he falls into any trouble or perplexity, whatsoever it may be and howsoever grievous it may be, immediately he shall either be delivered by Thee or be comforted by Thee; for Thou never forsakest him who trusts in Thee.

It is very hard to find a friend so faithful and so true that he will persevere with his friends in all his troubles; but Thou, Lord, art most faithful in all things, and none other can be found like Thee. O how that soul well savored spiritual things who said: 'My mind is established in God, and is fully grounded in Him.' Truly if it were so with me, the dread of man should not so quickly enter into me, and other men's words should not so soon move me.

Who may foresee all things? Or who may prevent all evils that are to come? And yet if things foreseen oftentimes do great hurt, what shall those things do that are not foreseen? But why have not I, wretch, better seen to myself? And why have I so readily believed other men's sayings? Truly, because we are men, and that but frail men, though we are esteemed and thought by many to be as angels in our conversation. Whom may I believe but only Thee? Thou art the Truth that deceivest no man, and mayst not be deceived. And on the other side, every man is a liar, weak and unstable, and sliding, most especially in words, so that scarcely may that be believed which seems on the surface to be true.

I am taught with my own hurt, and would to God it might be as a warning to me and not to my greater folly! Some say to me, 'Beware! Beware! Keep close to yourself what I shall show you.' And when I keep it close and believe it to be secret, he cannot be secret in what he himself desired, but immediately he betrays both himself and me, and goes his way. From such tales and from such unstable men, Lord, defend me, that I fall not into their hands, and that I never commit such things. A true and stable word, Lord, give unto my mouth, and a deceitful tongue drive far away from me; for that which I would not have others do to me, I ought to beware that I do not to any other.

O how good and how peaceful is it to keep silence of other men's words and deeds, and not to give full credence till the truth is tried; not to readily report to others all that we hear or see, and not to be moved with every blast of words; to open our heart fully but to very few; to seek Thee always who art the beholder of man's heart, and to desire that all things in us, inwardly and outwardly, may be fulfilled according to Thy will!

How sure a thing is it also for the keeping of heavenly grace to flee the conversation of worldly people all that we may, and not to desire things that seem outwardly to be pleasant and enjoyable; but with all the study of our heart to seek such things as bring fervor of spirit and amendment of life. A virtue known and repeatedly praised has been truly a great hurt to many persons; and on the contrary, a grace kept in silence and not readily reported to others has been very profitable to some in this frail life that is full of temptation and secret envy.

CHAPTER XV

Of Patient Suffering Of Injuries And Wrongs, And Who Is Truly Patient

'My son, what is it you say? Why do you thus complain? Cease, cease! Complain no more! Consider the tribulations of the saints, and you shall well see that it is very little that you suffer for Me! You have not yet suffered to the shedding of your blood, and truly you have suffered little in comparison with those who have suffered so many things for Me in time past, and who have been so strongly tempted, so grievously troubled, and so many ways proved. It behoves you, therefore, to remember the great grievous things that others have suffered for Me, that you may the more easily bear your little griefs. And if they seem not little to you, see that it is not your impatience that is the cause; but nevertheless, whether they are little or great, study always to bear them patiently without grudging or complaining, if you may. The better that you can dispose yourself to suffer them, the wiselier you do, and the more merit shall you have; and by reason of your good custom and of your good will your burden shall be the lighter.

'You should never say: "I cannot suffer this thing of such a person, nor is it for me to suffer it; he has done me great wrong and accuses me of that which I never thought; but of another man I will suffer as I shall think." Such kinds of sayings are not good, for they consider not the virtue of patience, nor by whom it shall be rewarded; but they consider rather the persons and the offences done unto them.

'Therefore he is not truly patient who will suffer only as much as he will, and of whom he will; for a truly patient man heeds not by whom he suffers, whether by his superior, or by his fellow who is equal to him, or of any other who is under him;

nor whether he is a good and holy man, or an evil and unworthy man. But whenever any adversity or wrong falls unto him, whatsoever it be, and by whomsoever it be, and howsoever often it be, he takes all thankfully, as from the hand of God, and accounts it as a precious gift and a great benefit; for he knows well that there is nothing that a man may suffer for God that may pass without great merit.

'Therefore, be ready to battle, if you would have the victory. Without battle you may not come to the reward of patience, and if you will not suffer, you refuse to be rewarded. Wherefore, if you will be rewarded, resist strongly and suffer patiently. For without labor no man may come to rest, and without battle no man may come to victory.'

Dear Lord, make possible to me by grace that which is impossible to me by nature! Thou knowest well that I may little suffer, and that I am immediately cast down with a little adversity. Wherefore I beseech Thee that trouble and adversity may hereafter, for Thy name, be beloved and desired by me; for truly, to suffer and to be vexed for Thee is very good and profitable to the health of my soul.

CHAPTER XVI

That A Man Shall Not Be Overmuch Cast Into Heaviness Though He Happen To Fall Into Some Faults

'My son, patience and meekness in adversity please me more than much consolation and devotion in prosperity. Why are you so heavy for a little word said or done against you? If it had been more, you should not have been moved therewith. But let it now overpass; it is not the first, and it shall not be the last if you live long. You are manful enough so long as no adversity falls to you; and you can well give counsel and well can you comfort and strengthen others with your words. But when adversity knocks at your own door, you fail immediately both of counsel and strength. Behold well, therefore, your great frailty of which you have daily experience in little temptations. Nevertheless it is for your spiritual health that such things, and similar things are allowed to come to you.

'Intend in your heart to do the best that is in you to do, and then when such tribulations shall happen to fall unto you, although it grieves you, yet let it not wholly overthrow you, nor let it long remain with you. And at the least suffer it patiently although you may not suffer it gladly.

Moreover, though you are loathe to hear such things, and though you feel great indignation thereat in your heart, yet thrust yourself down low in your own sight and suffer no inordinate word to pass out of your mouth, whereby any other might be hurt. Then all such indignation shall be immediately assuaged and soon appeased in you. And then also that which before was taken as so great heaviness to you, shall immediately be made sweet and pleasant in your sight. For yet I live, ready to help you and to comfort you more than ever I did before, if you will wholly trust in Me and devoutly call to Me for help.

'Be quiet in heart; prepare yourself to yet more sufferance. For it is not all lost though you feel yourself often troubled or grievously tempted. Think you are a man and not God; a fleshly man and no angel. How may you always stand in one state of virtue when that was not given to angels in heaven, nor to any of my saints? I am He who raises up them who are sorrowful to health and comfort; and lifts them up who know their unstableness, to be established in the sight of My Godhead forever.'

Lord, blessed is Thy holy word! It is sweeter to my mouth than honeycomb! What should I do in all my troubles and heaviness if Thou didst not sometimes comfort me with Thy sweet and wholesome words? Therefore it matters not what trouble or adversity I suffer here for Thee, so that I may in the end come to the port of everlasting salvation. Give me a good end and a blessed passage out of this world. Have mind on me, my Lord and my God, and direct me by a straight and ready way into Thy kingdom, I beseech Thee.

CHAPTER XVII

That We Shall Put All Our Confidence In God When Evil Words Are Spoken To Us

'My son', saith our Lord, 'stand strongly and trust faithfully in Me. What are words but wind? They fly in the air but they hurt never a stone on the ground; and if you know yourself not guilty, think that you will suffer gladly such words for God. It is but a little thing for you to suffer sometimes a hasty word since you are not yet able to suffer hard strokes. But why is it that so little a thing goes so near your heart, but that you are yet carnal, and heed to please men more than you should? And because you dread to be despised you will not gladly be reproved for your offenses, and you search therefore busily and with great study how you may be excused. But behold yourself well and you shall see that the world yet lives in you, and a vain love also to please man.

When you refuse to be rebuked and punished for your faults, it appears evident that you are not yet really meek and that you are not yet dead to the world, nor the world to you.

'But hear My words, and you shall not need to care for the words of ten thousand men. Lo, if all things were said against you that might be most maliciously and untruly feigned, what should they hurt if you simply allow them to overpass and go away? Truly, no more than a straw under your foot, and one hair of your head they might not take from you. But he who has not a man's heart within him, and sets not God before the eye of his soul, is soon moved with a sharp word; when he who trusts in Me, and will not stand in his own judgement, shall be free from all the dread of man. For I am the judge who knows all secrets. I know how everything is done, and I know also both him who does the wrong and him to whom it is done. Of Me this thing is wrought; and by My consent it has come about. So that the thoughts of men's hearts may be known, when the time comes, I shall reveal both the innocent and the guilty; but first, through My righteous examination, I will prove them both. The witness of man oftentimes deceives, but My judgement is true and shall not be subverted. And although it is sometimes hidden and known but to few, yet it is ever true and errs not; nor may it err, though in the sight of some unwise persons it seems not so.

'Therefore in every doubt it behoves you to come to Me and not to lean much to your own reason, but with everything that I shall send you to be content; for a righteous man is never troubled with anything that I shall allow to fall unto him. Insomuch that though a thing were untruly spoken against him, he should not much care for it, nor should he much joy, though he were sometimes reasonably excused. For he thinks always that I am He who searches man's heart, and that I judge not according to the outward appearance; for oftentimes that shall be found in My sight worthy to be blamed which in man's sight seems much worthy to be praised.'

O Lord God, most righteous judge, strong and patient, who knowest the frailty and the malice of man, be my strength and my whole comfort in all necessities; for my own conscience, Lord, suffices me not, and Thou knowest in me that which I know not. And therefore in every reproof I ought always to humble myself, and patiently to suffer all things in charity according to Thy pleasure. Forgive me, Lord, as often as I have not so done, and give me grace of greater sufferance in time to come. Thy mercy is more profitable, and a more sure way for me to the getting of pardon and forgiveness of my sins, than a trust in my own works, through defence of my darkened conscience. And though I dread not my conscience, yet I may not therefore justify myself; for if Thy mercy is taken away, no man may be justified nor appear righteous in Thy sight.

CHAPTER XVIII

How All Grievous Things In This Life Are Gladly To Be suffered For Winning Of The Life That Is To Come

'My son', saith our Lord, 'be not broken by impatience with the labor that you have taken for My sake; nor allow tribulation to cast you into despair, nor into unreasonable heaviness and anguish in any way. But be comforted and strengthened in every tribulation by My promises and behests, for I am able and of sufficient power to reward you and My other servants abundantly, more than you think or desire. You shall not labor long here, nor always be grieved with heaviness. Await for awhile My promises, and you shall soon see an end of all your troubles. An hour shall come when all your labors and troubles shall cease. And truly that hour is at hand, for all is short that passes with time.

'Therefore, continue to do as you do; labor busily and faithfully in My vineyard and I shall shortly be your reward. Write, read, sing, mourn, be still and pray, and suffer adversity gladly, for the kingdom of God is worth more than all these things, and much greater things than they are. Peace shall come one day that is known to Me, and that shall not be a day of this life, but a day everlasting, with infinite clearness, steadfast peace, and secure rest, without ending. And then you shall not say: "Who shall deliver me from this body of death?" Nor shall you need to cry: "Woe is to me, that my coming to the kingdom of God is thus prolonged!" For death shall then be destroyed, and health of body and of soul shall be without end; insomuch that no manner of unrestfulness shall be, but blessed joy, and sweetest and most fair company.

'O if you saw the everlasting reward of My saints in heaven, in how great joy and glory they are who sometime seemed to be as men despisable in the world, you should immediately humble yourself low to the ground; and you should rather covet to be subject to all men than to have sovereignty over any one person. You should not desire to have mirth and solace in this world, but rather bear with tribulation and pain; and you should then account it as a great grace to be taken as nothing among the people. O if these things savored well to you and deeply pierced into your heart, you should not once dare complain for any manner of trouble that should befall you! Are not all painful things and most grievous labors gladly to be suffered for the joys everlasting? Yes, truly;

for it is no little thing to win or lose the kingdom of God!

'Lift up your face therefore unto heaven, and behold how all My saints who are with Me there had in this world great battle and conflict; and now they joy with Me and are comforted in Me, and are sure to abide with Me and to dwell with Me in My everlasting kingdom.'

CHAPTER XIX

How A Man Should Rest In God Above All Things

Above all things and in all things, rest, my soul, in your Lord God, for He is the eternal rest of all angels and saints.

Grant me, Lord, special grace to rest in Thee above all creatures, above all health and fairness, above all glory and honor, above all dignity and power, above all wisdom and policy, above all riches and crafts, above all gladness of body and of soul, above all fame and praising, above all sweetness and consolation, above all hope and promise, above all merit and desire, above all gifts and rewards that Thou mayst give or send besides Thyself, and above all joy and mirth that man's heart or mind may feel. And also above all angels and all the company of heavenly spirits, above all things visible and invisible, and above all things that are not Thyself.

For Thou, Lord God, art most good, most high, most mighty, most sufficient and full of goodness; most sweet, most comforting, most fair, most loving, most noble, and most glorious above all things; in whom all goodness and perfection is, has been, and ever shall be. And therefore whatsoever Thou givest me besides Thyself, it is little and insufficient to me; for my heart may not rest nor fully be pacified so that it ascend above all gifts and above all manner of things that are created, unless in Thee.

O my Lord, most loving spouse, most pure lover and governor of every creature! Who shall give me wings of perfect liberty that I may fly high and rest in Thee! O when shall I fully tend to Thee, and see and feel how sweet Thou art? When shall I gather myself together in Thee so perfectly that I shall not, for Thy love, feel myself, but Thee alone, above myself and above all bodily things, and that Thou shalt visit me in such a way as Thou dost visit Thy faithful lovers?

Now I often mourn and complain of the miseries of this life, and with sorrow and woe bear them with very great heaviness. For many evil things happen daily in this life which oftentimes trouble me and greatly darken my understanding. They hinder me greatly and put my mind from

Thee, and so encumber me many ways so that I cannot have a free mind and pure desire toward Thee, nor have the sweet embracings that to Thy blessed saints are always present. Wherefore I beseech Thee, Lord, that the sighings and the inward desires of my heart, along with my manifold desolations, may somewhat move Thee and incline Thee to hear me.

O Lord, the light and brightness of everlasting glory, the joy and comfort of all Thy children walking and laboring as pilgrims in the wilderness of this world! My heart cries to Thee by still desires without voice, and my silence speaks unto Thee and says thus: 'How long tarrieth my Lord God to come? Truly, I trust that He will shortly come to me, His poorest servant, and comfort me and make me joyous and glad in Him, and deliver me from all anguish and sorrow.

'Come, Lord, come, for without Thee I have no glad day nor hour! Thou art all my joy and gladness, and without Thee my soul is barren and void. I am a wretch, and as though imprisoned and bound with fetters, till Thou, through the light of Thy gracious presence, consent to visit me and to refresh me, to bring me again to liberty of spirit, and to show Thy favorable and lovely countenance unto me. Let others seek what they will, but truly there is nothing that I will seek or that shall please me but Thou, my Lord God, my hope and everlasting health.'

And I shall not cease my prayer till Thy grace return to me again, and Thou speak inwardly to my soul and say thus: 'Lo, I am here! I am come to you for you have called Me! Your tears and the desire of your heart, your meekness and your contrition have bowed Me down and brought Me to you!'

And I shall say again: 'Lord, I have called Thee and I have desired to have Thee; I am ready to forsake all things for Thee. Thou hast first stirred me to seek Thee, wherefore bless Thee always who hast showed such goodness and mercy to me. What has Thy servant, Lord, more to do or say, but that he humble himself before Thy majesty and ever have in mind his own iniquity? There is none like to Thee, Lord, in heaven or in earth. Thy works are good, Thy judgements are righteous, and by Thy providence all things are governed. Wherefore to Thee be everlasting joy and glory! And I humbly beseech Thee that my body and soul, my heart and tongue, and all Thy creatures, may always laud Thee and bless Thee.'

CHAPTER XX

Of The Day Of Eternity And Of The Miseries Of This Life

O blessed mansion of the heavenly city! Most clear day of eternity! that the night may not darken, but the high Truth that God is illumines and reveals, always merry, always secure, and never changing its state into the contrary. Would to God that that day might now appear and shine upon us, and that these temporal things were at an end! That blessed day shines to saints in heaven with everlasting brightness and clarity, but to us pilgrims on earth it shines but afar off, as through a mirror or glass. The heavenly citizens know well how joyous that day is. But we exiles weep and wail the bitterness and weariness of this day, that is, of this present life; short and evil, full of sorrows and anguishes, where man is oftentimes defiled with sin, encumbered with passions, inquieted with dreads, bound with obligations, busied with vanities, blinded with errors, overtaxed with labors, vexed with temptations, overcome with delights and pleasures of the world, and grievously tormented sometimes with penury and need.

O when shall the end come of all these miseries! And when shall I be delivered from the bondage of sin! When shall I, Lord, have my mind only on Thee, and fully be made glad and merry in Thee! When shall I be free without hindrance and in perfect liberty without grief of body and of soul? When shall I have peace without trouble, peace within and without and on every side, steadfast and sure? O Lord! when shall I stand and behold Thee, and have full sight and contemplation of Thy glory? When shalt Thou be to me all in all? When shall I be with Thee in Thy kingdom, that Thou hast ordained for Thy elect people from the beginning?

I am left here poor and as an alien in the land of my enemies, where daily are battles and great misfortunes. Comfort my exile, assuage my sorrow, for all my desire cries to Thee! It is to me a grievous burden, whatsoever the world offers me here for my solace. I desire to have inward fruition in Thee, but I cannot attain thereto! I covet to cleave fast to heavenly things, but temporal things and passions unmortified pull me always downward. In mind I would be above all temporal things; but whether I will or not, I am compelled through my own fault to be subject unto my flesh. Thus I, most wretched man, fight in myself and am made grievous to myself, while my spirit desires to be upward and my flesh downward. O what I suffer inwardly, when in my mind I behold heavenly things and immediately a great multitude of carnal thoughts enter into my soul! Therefore, Lord, do not be long from me and depart not in Thy wrath from me, Thy servant!

Send to me the light of Thy grace and break down in me all carnal thoughts. Send forth the darts of Thy love and break therewith all fantasies of sin. Help me, Thou everlasting Truth, that no worldly vanity hereafter have power in me! Come also, Thou heavenly sweetness, and let all bitterness of sin flee far from me!

Pardon me, and mercifully forgive me when I think in my prayer of anything but of Thee! I confess for truth that in time past I have used myself very unstably therein, and many times I am not there where I stand or sit, but rather I am where my thoughts lead me. For that comes into my mind which by custom pleases me best to think upon; and where my thought is accustomed to be, there is that which I love. Wherefore it has been said: 'Where your treasure is, there is your heart.' Wherefore if I love heaven, I speak gladly of heavenly things, and of such things as are of God and pertain most to His honor and to the glorifying and worshiping of His holy name. And if I love the world I joy immediately at worldly felicity, and sorrow at its adversity. If I love the flesh, I imagine oftentimes that which pleases the flesh; and if I love my soul, I delight much to speak and to hear of things that are to my soul's health. And so whatsoever I love, of that I gladly hear and speak, and bear the images of that often in my mind.

Blessed is that man who, for the Lord, forgets

all created things and learns truly to overcome himself; and who with fervor of spirit has victory over the flesh, so that in a clean and pure conscience he may offer his prayers to Thee, and be worthy to have company of blessed angels, all earthly things excluded from him and fully set apart.

Chapter XXI

Of The Desire Of Everlasting Life And Of The Great Reward That Is Promised To Them Who Strongly Fight Against Sin

'My son, when you feel that a desire of everlasting bliss is given to you and that you covet to go out of the tabernacle of your mortal body, that you might clearly behold Me, beyond all forms, open your heart and with all the desire of your soul take that holy inspiration. And yield most large thanks to the high goodness of God who so worthily does to you, so benignly visits you, so burningly stirs you, and so strongly bears you up, that through your own burden you fall not down to earthly desires. Think not that that desire comes from yourself or by your own work-

ing, but rather that it comes by the gift of grace
and by a lovely beholding of God upon you. Such
grace is given in order that you should profit
thereby in meekness and virtue, and that you
should also prepare yourself to be ready against
another time, for battles that are to come; and the
more surely to cleave to God with all the desire
and affection of your heart, and to study with all
your power how you may most purely and most
devoutly serve Him.

'Take heed of this common proverb: "The fire
often burns, but the flame does not ascend without some smoke." So likewise, the desire of some
men draws to heavenly things, and yet they are
not all free from the smoke of carnal affections,
and therefore they do not always seek purely for
the honor and love of God that which they so
desirously ask of Him. Such oftentimes is your
own desire which you so importunately ask, for
that desire is not clean and perfect that is mixed
with your own commodity. Ask therefore not that
which is delectable and profitable to you, but that
which is acceptable and honor to Me; for if you
will do well and judge aright, you shall prefer My
ordinance and My will before all your desire, and
before all things that may be desired besides Me.

'I know well your desire. You would now be in
the liberty of the glory of the sons of God; now
your everlasting home and country full of joy and
glory, delights you much; but that hour comes

not yet. For there is yet another time to come, a time of labor and of proof. You desire to be fulfilled with the high goodness in heaven but you may not yet come thereto. I am the full reward of man. Await Me till I shall come and you shall have Me to your reward.

'You are yet to be proved here upon earth and more thoroughly to be tried in many things. Some comfort shall be given you, but the fullness thereof shall not yet be granted. Therefore, be comforted in Me, and be strong, as well in doing, as in suffering things contrary to your will. It behoves you to be changed into a new man; and you must oftentimes do that which you would not do, and that which you would do, you must forsake and leave undone.

'That which pleases others shall go well forward, and that which pleases you shall find no favor. That which other men say shall be well heard, and that which you say shall be disregarded. Others shall ask and have what they ask; you shall ask and be denied. Others shall be great and have great applause and praise from the people; and of you no word shall be spoken. To others, this office or that shall be committed, and you shall be judged unprofitable in everything. For these and other similar things nature will murmur and grudge, and you shall have a great battle in yourself if you bear them secretly in your heart without complaining and contradicting. Nevertheless, in such things and other similar things, my faithful servants are proved: how they can deny themselves and how they can in all things break their own wills.

'There is nothing that you shall need so much to overcome yourself in as to learn to be contented not to be valued in the world, and to suffer such things as are most contrary to your will; especially when such things as, in your sight, seem unprofitable are commanded to be done. But, My son, consider well the speedy end, and the great reward; and then you shall feel no grief or pain in all your labors, but the most sweet comfort of the Spirit through your good will. And for that little will which you forsake here, you shall always have your will in heaven where you shall have all that you can desire.

'There, your will shall be ever one with My will, and it shall covet no strange or private things. There, no man shall resist you, no man shall complain of you, no man shall hinder or withstand you; but all things that you can desire shall be present there, and shall fulfill all the powers of your soul unto the full. There shall I yield glory for reproofs, and a robe of praise for your sorrows, and for the lowest place here, a seat in heaven forever. There shall appear the fruit of obedience; the reward of your labor of penance shall be joy, and your humble subjection shall be gloriously crowned.

'Bow you now, therefore, meekly under man's

hand. Regard little who says this, or who commands this to be done; but with all your study take heed that whether your superior, or your fellow, or any other lower than you, ask anything of you or will anything to be done by you, that you take it always to the best, and with a glad will study to fulfill it. Let this man seek this thing, and another that; and let this man joy in this thing and another in that, whatsoever it may be; and let them be applauded and praised a thousand times; but joy you neither in this thing nor in that, but only in your own contempt and despising, and in My will to be fulfilled; and, whether it is by life or death, that I may always be praised and honored in you and by you.'

CHAPTER XXII

How A Man Who Is Desolate
Ought To Offer Himself Wholly To God

Lord, holy Father, Thou art blessed now and forever! For as Thou wilt so it is done and that which Thou dost is always good. Let me, Thy poorest and most unworthy servant, joy in Thee and not in myself nor in anything else besides Thee. For Thou, Lord, art my gladness! Thou art my hope, my crown, my joy, and all my honor!

What has Thy servant but that which he has from Thee, and that without his deserving! All things are Thine that Thou hast given and made.

I am poor, and have been in trouble and in pain ever from my youth; and my soul has been in great heaviness with weeping and tears, and sometimes it has been troubled in itself through manifold passions that come of the world and of the flesh. Wherefore, Lord, I desire that I may have from Thee the joy of inward peace, and the repose of Thy chosen children who are fed and nourished by Thee in the light of heavenly comforts; but without Thy help I cannot come thereto. If Thou, Lord, give peace, or if Thou give inward joy, my soul immediately shall be full of heavenly melody, and be devout and fervent in Thy praisings. But if Thou withdraw Thyself from me as Thou hast sometimes done, then Thy servant may not run the way of Thy commandments as he did first; but he is compelled to bow his knees and to strike his breast, for it is not with him as it was before, when the light of Thy spiritual presence shone upon his forehead and he was defended under the shadow of Thy mercy from all perils and dangers.

O righteous Father, ever to be praised, the time is come that Thou hast ordained for Thy servant to be proved! And righteously is it done, that I shall now suffer somewhat for Thee. Now is the hour come that Thou hast known from the beginning: that Thy servant for a time should outwardly be regarded as nothing, and inwardly live to Thee; and that he should a little be despised in the sight of the world and be broken with passions and sickness, that he might afterward rise with Thee into a new light and be illumined and made glorious in the kingdom of God.

O holy Father, Thou hast ordained it so to be, and it is done as Thou hast commanded. This is Thy grace to Thy friend: to suffer and to be troubled in this world for Thy love, howsoever often it may be, and by whatsoever person it may be, and in whatsoever manner it is allowed to fall unto him. Nothing is done upon earth without Thy counsel and providence, nor without cause. O it is good to me, Lord, that Thou hast humbled me, that I may thereby learn to know Thy righteous judgements and put from me all manner of presumption and highness of heart. And it is very profitable to me that confusion has covered my face, that I may learn thereby to seek for help and succor of Thee, rather than of man. I have thereby learned to dread Thy secret and terrible judgement that scourges the righteous man with the sinner, but not without equity and justice.

I yield thanks to Thee that Thou hast not spared my sins, but hast punished me with scourges of love, and hast sent me sorrows and anguishes within and without, so that there is no creature under heaven who may comfort me but

Thou, Lord God, the heavenly physician of man's soul, who strikest and healest and bringest a man near unto bodily death, and after restorest him to health again, that he may thereby learn to know the littleness of his own power, and to trust the more fully in Thee.

Thy discipline is fallen upon me and Thy rod of correction hath taught me. Under that rod I wholly submit myself: strike my back and my bones as it shall please Thee, and make me to bow my crooked will unto Thy will; make me a meek and humble disciple as Thou hast sometimes done with me, that I may walk entirely according to Thy will. To Thee I commit myself and all mine to be corrected; for better it is to be corrected by Thee here, than in time to come. Thou knowest things to come, before they occur; and it is not necessary that any man teach Thee or warn Thee of anything that is done upon the earth. Thou knowest what is to my advantage, and how much tribulation helps to purge the rust of sin in me. Do with me according to Thy pleasure, and disdain not my sinful life, to none so well known as it is to Thee.

Grant me, Lord, to know that which is necessary to be known; to love that which is to be loved; to praise that which highly pleases Thee; to regard that which appears precious in Thy sight; and to refuse that which is vile before Thee. Do not allow me to judge according to my outward senses, nor to give judgement after the hearing of unwise men, but in a true judgement to discern things visible and invisible, and above all things always to search and follow Thy will and pleasure. The outward senses of men are often deceived in their judgements. And, likewise, the lovers of the world are deceived through loving only visible things.

What is a man the better simply because he is taken to be better? Truly nothing! For one deceitful man deceives another; one vain man deceives another; and a blind and feeble creature deceives another when he exalts him, and rather confounds him than praises him. For why? How much soever a man is in the sight of God, says the meek Saint Francis, so much he is, and no more; however holy and however virtuous he is taken to be in the sight of the people.

CHAPTER XXIII

That A Man Should Give Himself To Humble Bodily Labors When He Feels Himself Not Disposed To High Works Of Devotion

'My son, you may not always stand in the high fervent desire of virtue nor in the highest degree of contemplation, but you must of necessity sometimes descend to lower things, and against your will and with great weariness bear the burden of this corruptible body. For as long as you bear this body of death, you must feel some tediousness and grief of heart, and you shall oftentimes beweep and mourn the burden of your fleshly feelings and the contradiction of your body to the soul; for you may not, for the corruption thereof, persevere in spiritual studies and in heavenly contemplation as you would wish to do.

'Then it is good for you to flee to meek bodily labors and to exercise yourself in good outward works; and in a steadfast hope and trust to await My coming and My new heavenly visitations, and to bear your exile and the dryness of your heart patiently, till you shall be visited by Me again and be delivered from all tediousness and unquietness of mind. When I come I shall make you forget all your former labors and have inward rest and quietness of soul.

'I shall open before you the meadows of the scriptures, and you shall, with great gladness of heart, perceive them with a new and clearer understanding. Then shall you follow the way of My commandments, and you shall say with great spiritual gladness: "The sufferings of this time are not worthy to be compared with the coming glory that shall be revealed in us."'

CHAPTER XXIV

That All Our Hope And Trust Is To Be Put In God Alone

O Lord, what is the trust that I have in this life, or what is my greatest solace of all things under heaven? Is it not Thou, my Lord God, whose mercy is without measure? Where has it been well with me without Thee, or when has it not been well with me, Thou being present? I would rather be poor with Thee, than rich without Thee. I would rather be with Thee as a pilgrim in this world, than without Thee to be in heaven; for where Thou art there is heaven, and where Thou art not, there is both death and hell. Thou art to me all that I desire; and therefore it behoves me to sigh to Thee, to cry to Thee, and heartily to pray to Thee. I have nothing to trust in that may help me in my necessities but only Thee. For Thou art my hope, Thou art my trust, Thou art my comfort, and Thou art my most faithful helper in every need.

Man seeks that which is his, but Thou seekest my health and profit, and turnest all things into the best for me. If Thou send temptations and other adversities, Thou ordainest all to my profit, for Thou art wont by a thousand ways to prove Thy chosen people. In which proof Thou art no less to be lauded and praised, than if Thou hadst fulfilled them with heavenly comforts.

In Thee, Lord, therefore, I put my trust, and in Thee I bear patiently all my adversities; for I find nothing without Thee but unstableness and folly. I see well that the multitude of worldly friends profits not; that strong helpers may avail nothing; nor wise counselors give profitable counsel; nor cunning of doctors give consolation; nor riches deliver in time of need; nor secret place anything defend. For all things that seem to be ordained to man's solace in this world, if Thou art absent, are worth nothing; nor may they bring to man any true felicity. For Thou, Lord, art the end of all good things, the highness of life, and the profound wisdom of all creatures who are in heaven and in earth. Wherefore to trust in Thee above all things is the greatest comfort to all Thy servants. To Thee, therefore, the Father of mercy, do I lift up my eyes! In Thee, only, my Lord, my God, do I put my trust!

Bless and hallow my soul with Thy heavenly blessings, that it may be Thy dwelling place and the seat of Thy eternal glory; so that nothing may be found in me at any time that may offend the eye of Thy majesty. Behold me, Lord, according to the greatness of Thy goodness and Thy manifold mercies; and graciously hear the prayer of me, Thy poorest servant, outlawed and far exiled into the country of the shadow of death! Defend and keep me among the manifold perils and dangers of this corruptible life, and direct me through Thy grace by the ways of peace into the country of everlasting clearness without ending.

– Here ends the Third Book –